D0892065

FISHING

MORE THAN A PASSION

FISHING

MORE THAN A PASSION

MUSINGS & VERSE FROM
AN IOWA FISHERMAN

BEN CHIODO

PUBLISHING + DESIGN

ISBN: 978-1-7323526-1-2

Published and printed in the United States of America
by the Write Place, Inc. For more information, please contact:

the Write Place, Inc.
809 W. 8th Street, Suite 2
Pella, Iowa 50219
www.thewriteplace.biz

Cover and interior design by Michelle Stam, the Write Place, Inc.
Cover and interior artwork by Larry Anderson.

Copies of this book may be ordered online at Amazon
and BarnesandNoble.com.

View other Write Place titles at www.thewriteplace.biz.

ACKNOWLEDGMENTS

Larry Anderson is a close, close friend. Having any of his art in this book is a prize. He has surprised me many times, and I cherish his friendship.

PREFACE

This book is a little fishy...don't take it too seriously.

When I was six years old, I wanted to go fishing. Now, where I got that idea I couldn't tell you.

The guys I played with would go to the river, which was just a few blocks away. If you cut through a few yards, it may have been two blocks away, as the broken-winged crow flies. We would go under the bridge and fish next to the dam. The fish of the day consisted mostly of bullheads and carp. If we were lucky, maybe a walleye or an occasional crappie and bluegill.

But my mom was protective and didn't want me around water deeper than two inches unless she was close by. She would permit me to sit on a swing outside on the front porch. It was made out of an old board connected to rusty chains, hanging from an extended clothesline post. As I would swing, it would squeak and my mother could hear me from the kitchen. When she didn't hear this odd warning system, she would check on me. Usually, I'd be off to the river to fish.

We were not much on money. My dad was an Italian, the old-fashioned type. No fishing, no sports, no games. *Youa work, you no play games. You make money working, no sports.*

My mother was English, Irish, and Sioux Indian—a combination you don't come across every day. I had three sisters, and Mom was allowed to deal with them when it came to punishment. If I needed to be punished, Mom wasn't allowed to do so.

My dad was the only one to have that honor. She would tell Dad when I misbehaved, and he would pull off his strap. That belt was 20 feet long and could reach me no matter how far I ran.

When I would sneak off to fish, Mom wouldn't hear the swing and she'd come a-lookin'. I'd be below the bridge, fishing. The guys would bring my reel and line to give to me if I made it that far. My reel was a Coke bottle with a white string and a heavy sinker and hook attached. The line was wrapped around the bottle and would flow off when you cast. It worked for us and caught a lot of fish.

Even then, fishing was so much fun. I had to pay for taking off, though. My mother would come after me and yell, "Is my boy down there?" My friends would say no, but she knew they were lying. I'd run up the other side to beat her home—to no avail.

We had this willow tree in the backyard, and Mom would have me pull down my drawers for the whole neighborhood to see. When I gave her a willow limb, the whipping would begin. That hurt like sin. After she was done, she would tell me not to tell Dad, or it would be worse next time. Dad didn't want her to punish me, but she did what she preferred. I was inclined to believe her—you could bottoms up toasting that suggestion.

It wasn't too long before the willow tree had only four limbs left. A person who only fishes occasionally or only fishes for food would have a hard time understanding my desire and love for fishing in the face of this punishment. But even back then, I wanted to find that Big One, that once-in-a-lifetime catch. It's easier to win the lottery, unless your funds are available to go big-fish hunting.

Well, I swore to myself I wouldn't cry anymore. I would bear my bottom beatings, even though that was almost impossible to do. I didn't fully understand that my mother was afraid I would drown.

We were down to those four willows. The next time my butt was bare, I bent over and waited for some pain. Then I heard whimpering. My mother could no longer deliver. I won the argument, and I knew then that I had caught one of my biggest fish.

After that, Mom took me to the river herself and let me fish. We did this twice a week.

My occasional fishing trips didn't last long though. I got a job at the store across the street from our house, and it kept me busy six days a week and one half-day on Sunday. The small store was southside busy and kept me so. It had a wood floor, and dust became airborne. Whenever I finished cleaning the shelves, they were ready to be cleaned again.

Well, so much for my own love to fish. I have decided to write some prose and poetry on fishing—not serious and definitely not by the pros!

PART I

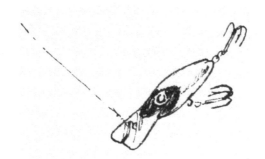

© ANDERSON...

PROSE

WHAT IS A FISHING BOOK ABOUT?

Is it about catching fish? No, it's about you. It's about your desire to catch fish. We all want to catch the Big One, but what are you willing to sacrifice? Will you withstand the rain, the cold, any storm? You'll try almost anything within reason. It's the same as buying tickets for the lotto and believing you will win.

NEVER FISH ALONE

Fishing should always be fun. Don't let it go any other way. Always take a partner and any child who wants to learn. You should never want to fish alone. Every day you can learn, and every day you will have something to share. Yes, we are all after the Big One—the struggle to get it on the shore or in the boat and the satisfaction of knowing you will never stop trying.

SO MUCH STRESS

There is so much stress in the world; you should always do something that relaxes you. If you enjoy fishing, that's your cure. Now, you have your own style and there are certain fish you like to catch. But most of all, you like fishing. What you catch should not make that much difference. It should be a release for you, and it will be the best medicine you or anyone can prescribe. The sounds that surround you while you're fishing will help relax you.

THE TROUBLE WITH CONFIDENCE

If you think you're good, that is not good enough. You should consider yourself the best, better than any man. Even if that is not true, you must believe in yourself. You have to believe that if there is only one fish in a lake, you will find it.

The truth is, though, you will always be good but never good enough. If you're number-one in your own mind, then your sanity should be in question. But don't let that stop you from believing in yourself.

MAPPING NEW LAKES

If you're going to fish a lake that is strange to you, acquire a map. Spot yourself and don't change your mind. Always pick four places on the lake using your depth map. Stay with your decision of where to fish.

If you find you're not catching in one of the planned areas, then go to the next, then the next. You might find yourself starting over again. Do not become discouraged. The worst thing you can do is doubt yourself. If you do, the fish have bagged you.

A PRESENT WRAPPED IN PURE ENJOYMENT

As long as you enjoy what you're doing, there is nothing that can ruin your day. Confucius said, "A day of fishing is better than a day at work." Or was that Caesar? Oh well, who cares? Whoever it was couldn't be completely far from the truth!

We take a lot of things for granted, but a good day of fishing is a gift—a present wrapped in pure enjoyment. And if you do take a child fishing and teach him some of your skills, God will keep you in His sight.

IF THERE'S WATER, THERE'S FISHING

No matter where you are, you will find a place to fish. Even the desert has water somewhere. Look and you shall fish.

But never look blind—there is always a prospect up the road.

Never fish any place without permission. If you see water, there has to be someone you can ask. If the answer is no, then there is a good reason. There always will be. Don't let it bother you. There is the next place, and so on, and so on...

What has a down has an up.

TOURNAMENT FISHING, PART 1

Tournament fishing can be fun. But if you think you're the best, you'll always find someone luckier.

Hang on to your jewels—someone out there has better tools. Your fishing equipment may not be up to date, but I haven't found a fish that cared. The one who created the better worm already placed it in the ground. People like you and I might not have been around.

MY FIRST FISHING EQUIPMENT

My first fishing string came in a ball of white—the only color you could find that wasn't thread. I would cast it off a rolled-on Coke bottle with a heavy weight and hook.

You could make a hook out of a hanger if you had a good file. Over the years, I've lost a lot of fish and had to learn to keep a tight string. We would catch carp, bullheads, catfish, and what else. A fish was a fish, and if you could eat it, it was on the dish. Salt and pepper, everyone's spices, commodities that we felt were a luxury.

You could buy a reel that held string and a rod for a lot of pennies, but who had that many?

If we couldn't fish ourselves, we liked to watch other people to see if they would catch a large fish. When the water was up and flowing fast, the big flathead catfish would slide off the bottom of the river, and people would catch them. I'd sure like to know what one tasted like. Back in the day, no one would give one away. I figured a person was lucky to catch one or two.

WHO KNEW FISH WERE THAT SMART?

Guess what: They, whoever "they" are, can make fishing lures out of rubber to fool the fish. Now, who knew fish were that smart? You could have fooled me.

You have colored line and line you can't see underwater with hooks you also can't see. Fancy lures of all types that can go deep or on top. We buy all this to catch fish, and then we think the fish is dumb! You want a fish to bite, so you pound him in the head with all this stuff.

Can you believe the fish at times are not hungry? A good fisherman doesn't really care, as long as he is enjoying himself. A thousand dollars of equipment doesn't catch fish—you do.

IF YOU CATCH EVERYTHING, WHERE'S THE FUN?

What is more fun and relaxing than sitting next to a pond and fishing? Even in the rain, you can't beat it. You can make a bobber out of a stick and watch it tickle. Until you find out how the fish bite on the action on that stick, you could lose a few. But, of course, that's the fun of fishing. If you catch everything, where's the fun? You can lie back and look to the heavens and thank God you're able to be there. There are many on this earth who can't walk to a pond and fish. Don't you wish you could take a day of fishing to all of them?

WORTH A MILLION DOLLARS

You have to love the look on a child's face when he or she catches a fish. Now, that's better than catching a Big One yourself. Children make it ten times the fun, and they just like being there and fishing.

Going fishing is one thing your whole family can enjoy. People are so busy now, making a living, it's no longer a family sport. One or the other has something else to do. They don't want to miss their favorite TV show.

How often does anyone in your family dig for worms? In fact, when did one of them put a worm on a hook? Our society has been drawn away from the simple and better things in our lives. We let it happen and don't even realize what we're missing. So you're spending a dollar in gas taking your family fishing: It's worth a million to watch them having fun. Now, that would make anyone's day. At least once a month, plan an outing with your family. They will enjoy it, *no question!*

TYPES OF FISHERMEN

There's the spray fisherman, who sprays his lures, his hands, his rods, his reels—anything he has—to catch a fish. He sprays his trolling motor, his boat, and his wife for good measure.

Then you have the prayer fisherman, the sign-of-the-cross fisherman, and last but definitely not least, the hundred-rod-and-reel fisherman, who has different bait for each and a lot of spray. He has to buy a new pole because he steps on the ones he keeps underfoot in his boat.

A THOUSAND WAYS TO CATCH A FISH

A true fisherman has to have a boat that not only leads him to the fish, but also has a thousand ways to catch them (except for dynamite). If that was legal, he'd have it onboard. For a fish not having any brains, we sure go to a lot of trouble and expense to catch them.

THIS BOAT YOU HAVE WORKED TWENTY YEARS TO BUY

Now, you need a boat that has swivel seats that go up and down and all around. You never know which direction that fish is going to turn you when he catches you. Now, if you have a trolling motor that reads your thoughts, you don't much care which way the fish pulls. I should catch such a fish!

If you're whale fishing, I would have to re-write a few of my suggestions. Some boats cost more than a home, and I can see a true fisherman wanting to live in his boat, abandoning his family and all obligations. Of course, that is not really true. A good and true fisherman goes when he can and takes who he can with him. It doubles your enjoyment when you take another person along. There are those who like to fish alone, though. I think they find it easier to collect their thoughts and relax. Fishing is the best stress releaser.

Now, back to this boat you have worked twenty years to buy. This boat has a motor that will bring the boat above the water if you put out your arms. This motor not only flies, you can go from Point A to Point B in seconds. If you're on a fish, Joe Blow is not going to beat you to your spot. If you're in a tournament, you fly and fly alone. It's embarrassing to be passed by in a tournament situation—and to think another in your competition might pass you by. You never want to see a grown man cry.

When you catch that fish, it goes directly to the live well. There's to be no fish that hit the carpet. Who wants a fish smelling up his boat? Now that you have caught that first fish, you put your trolling motor on attack mode, and it will stay in the area and smell out your next prey. You might as well throw your line over the side and take a nap. If your next catch bites, your reel drag will tell you and you can take it aboard—only if you feel up to it.

THAT DARN JOE BLOW

Now you have a fish on the hook and that darn Joe Blow is passing by. Bad timing. You'd rather lose the fish than let him see you're on fish. You're going to sit back down with your rod in the water and wave.

You yell, "Got any fish?"

Of course, he'll say, "Just some little ones. How about you?"

You tell him, "Oh, I'm just enjoying the day. Good luck."

Like he'll believe you care. Now you're taking your line in and the fish is gone. *Just part of the game,* you think. Fishing is so much fun, and telling fish lies is not really lying. God only knows you're expected to do that. Fish stories are part of the fun.

ANOTHER FISH STORY

Well, now it's time for your boat to find some structure. You go to your boat's computer memory of the lake, and it tells you there's all this structure in a couple miles. You hear the fish are biting on black worms with a blue curly tail. Sure, another fish story. So, you're going to go with a blue worm with an orange tail. Think your mama raised a fool?

You pull out your 100-pound worm box with every color worm and weight. *Eeny, meeny, miney, moe, which one will make me the pro?* Maybe a crawdad or an eel type.

Well, you know you can catch fish on anything.

TOURNAMENT FISHING, PART 2

Fishing in a tournament does not appeal to everyone. There will be times you lose the fun. The competition can be overwhelming. To fish in a tournament, you've got to love a contest. You've got to love fishing.

When you're on fish, a tournament is just another day of fun fishing.

Don't you just hate it when you see a boat parked on fish? You've been searching for an hour and they're pulling in fish one after the other. Happy for them—not! There are days when it is hard to find fish that are feeding, and you need to tease them.

THE TREE LIMB

Do you remember the tree limb? In days past, you would stick your string and hook inside the river bank with your bait. When the fish bit, he would hook himself. You could catch some big fish that way. You think to yourself, *What fun is that?* Well, the joy in this is what's on your string and how big it is. In checking your lines and having to wait and see. Never been much on waiting for anything. You've got to like fishing. It's much better to go with a couple of others if you spend a night out fishing.

WHY FISHERMEN LIVE LONGER

Did you know fishermen live longer? They don't want to die before they catch the Big One. When we say BIG ONE, we want it to be a record fish.

Then the biggest fish is caught by a child playing next to the water with her or his little pole. That's great, but it doesn't give me a picture with it on my line.

BEAUTY OF THE BAMBOO POLE

What proven fisherman hasn't used a bamboo pole? I've seen some of the better fishermen sneak up to a bush in the water with a bamboo pole so they can reach out and not chase away the Big One. Anything that has proven to be a fish puller in the last hundred years is okay equipment in the pro world. It's so much fun when a fish comes out from under structure to hit your hook on the end of a bamboo pole.

CATCHING A FISH WITH DANIEL BOONE

There is nothing better than catching a fish with Daniel Boone. Wouldn't care to show my age, but I've seen and enjoyed the show—farmers in their underwear, flat back, butt covered, catching fish. A few would walk from upstream to the ones who were waiting down the way with gunnysacks and nets to catch anything that happened to come by. Some would unbutton—open up the top of their underwear to catch something. Bottles of beer were placed on the bank to celebrate success or commiserate failure. It made no difference when fun was the sport. You don't think it's a sight, a sixty-year-old jumping up and down in the water?

Fish were the best to eat then. The word "pollution" wasn't an issue. It was uncommon to find hundreds of dead fish in the streams. They didn't die from horse manure on the crops.

TURTLE SNATCHING

Then there is turtle snatching. Turtle is a delicacy few have experienced, and many have not tasted. Could you reach under the water, close to the side, and snatch a turtle bare-handed?

Guess what, join the no-way crowd! A turtle can snap off your "I'm-number-one" finger. There is, I guess, a way to do it—but I never cared to learn.

Turtle meat, and there are a couple of different kinds, is like eating the proverbial chicken. I think it has chicken beat. And, yeah, I realize you don't find it on the menu. Yes, I know you can't find a "turtle snatcher" in your phone directory. So? If you look long and hard, just maybe you can find some turtle meat. Never say "impossible" or "improbable." Those are two words that have no place in a believer's vocabulary. I would never reach under a log for a turtle, though, without iron gloves.

TOP-WATER FISHING

Top-water fishing, it can't get any more exciting than that! What can hit on the bottom can hit on the top. Don't take it for granted—just believe it or not. If you miss the first strike, go back; the next hit may be successful.

REMEMBER THE FROG DAYS?

They have lures that buzz, whistle, and spin. Soon, you will be able to buy dynamite with a twisty tail and a deep-diving bill. Remember the frog days? You could catch frogs with a piece of red ribbon and a hook.

Frogs make good bait if you know how to hook one up. Was it the feet, back, or mouth? I mean, what did a frog ever do to you? All they do is *urp, burp,* and *slurp.*

Now, frog fishing takes a man with patience—an individual who can watch four children and a football game at the same time. I mean, you might as well get a beer out of the cooler and relax as the fish takes *urp, burp,* and *slurp* to deeper water. When the line stops, wait a couple minutes and let her move out again. Then set your hook.

The battle is on. Oh, how you longed for the fight to be on! Darn, don't you like it when a play comes to pay, or when the left meets the right, or when the horse comes before the cart? I do believe that's when the fish lands onshore.

EVERYONE LIKES TO EAT WALLEYE

It seems everyone likes to eat walleye, and they are fun to catch. People like to troll for them. You can go forward, and you can go backward. Minnow-type bait is best, and the advantage in trolling is you have an opportunity to hook all kinds of things. A stick for instance, hooked under a rock. Or a bush. Don't you hate it when you set the hook on one of those? No one likes losing a lure, especially when it's the only one catching fish. Buy two of your favorite lures if you can afford it.

That reminds me of a place where I contributed several lures for fishing small-mouth. You would snag in this one area where the fish had their meetings, and there was no way of getting your best lure back. This place was by a small overflow, and the small-mouth loved it. You always left a lure or two behind.

Doggone, it would bring a priest to his wits' end! I couldn't tell you how many people left lures behind after fishing there. One day, I said to myself, "If I make plans to fish here again, I'm going to challenge that snag with a grabbing hook and rope."

I carried out my plan sooner than I thought I would. I parked my old four-wheeler on the hill, as close as I safely could to the edge, and threw my hook into the snag. Caught it on the first throw, went back to the old wheel clutch, and proceeded to move. In those days, you manually set the wheels into four-wheel one at a time outside the truck. I had my fingers crossed and hoped the rope was thick enough. The few people that were there went to a distant shelter. They looked at me oddly anyway. More power to me, I reckoned. I slowly move the old banger, wondering if this action was stupidity or a good idea.

Here comes the instrument of my hatred: Some son, or sons of the devil's dreams, had planted a box spring in the center of the fishing hole. It was full of lures—some dating back to Lincoln's inauguration.

Well, was that satisfying or what?

THE DOWNSIDE TO FISHING

Now, there is a downside to fishing. What if, just saying, there's a possibility you might not catch a fish? Then you go back to the old adage: "A bad day of fishing is, and will always be, better than a day at work." I think President Lincoln said something like that.

NO EXCUSE TO NOT GO FISHING

You have winter gear, summer gear, and rain gear. You have no excuse to not go fishing. If your spouse says no because you could be fishing in a storm, you might want to stay home and wait for better conditions. A fishing rod in your hand when there's lightning is not a condition—it's a poor decision.

You'll want to have a lifelong understanding with your other half about your fishing trips. If you can't go fishing, there's golf or just chasing after other pleasures. Of course, a true fisherman will have his grass cut, bed made, dishes cleaned, and socks off the floor. The plan-ahead fishing person always sends their spouse a love card, or a box of candy, or maybe a rose once a month. You don't want to spend too much—lures are expensive. But if you go after your other half with the same enthusiasm as you do fishing, your life may go much easier when fishing days come around. Remember: A love card you found, fishing abounds.

WHEN THE CURTAIN GOES UP

Don't ever get lazy or lackadaisical. Keep up with what's happening in the fishing world, especially in your interest area. You can't buy every new thing that claims to be the perfect fish attractor. You have to stage yourself. Only go on when the curtain goes up for your act. Remember, you'll always have your turn. It could be just around the corner. Consequently, stay in good health and do what you consider fun, within reason, every day. That's the stress-free way. And a reminder: If you can take a kid or children fishing, God will definitely smile on you. That holds true with all you do. Our hearts know when we have gone out of our way to help another person. You might not get the credit, but "what goes around" and so on. You be the judge.

FLY FISHING, PART 1

What about fly fishing? Doesn't it look easy and fun? It does take a lot of practice—stay away from bushes and trees when you are trying to learn. Use a small fly so it won't hurt as bad when you hook your butt.

When you're waving that pole around, be sure you are in a low-bird area—not that I would know the best places or have seen a bird catch a fly. But I did catch a bat when swinging a fly once, when it was close to dark. True story!

A fly fisherman does not pass up a chance to salmon fish along streams at a certain time of the year. Can't you just imagine fighting with a large salmon using your limp fly pole? Catching a small fish with fly fishing equipment is a load of fun, so can't you envision how a salmon would pull against your fly pole? A split bamboo pole with a reel can be costly, but it will last for a lifetime of enjoyment. And to think, it can be used by your children and grandchildren. These poles and reels can be expensive, but their futures can be continuous. You pitch and twitch—you have to experience the excitement you feel when that fish comes up to taste your offering.

Always go to the restroom before you go fly fishing.

We think we're ready for that fish when he comes up for your offering, and maybe we are, but it will still throw you into an excited state. Try to keep your line fairly firm on your reel. Don't be in a big hurry. The fight is the fun. If you lose one, your life will continue until the next one.

ALWAYS BE PREPARED

Fishermen live longer, waiting for success and to get what they want out of fishing. You have got to have a rod and reel in your transportation. You never know when you'll happen upon water—you just have a feeling there could be something hiding. If you're not ready, those possible catches might just pass you by. Well, the words for that are, "Shame, shame, you're to blame". There are a lot of ponds to fish; just ask the landowner first.

Carry an old window screen with you. There could be some minnows accumulating somewhere close by. I can relate to cheap bait. There's nothing like a live minnow. You will never find a lure that can take its place. The fishing companies have come as close as they can, and they can't do it. Look at the expense we go through trying to keep the little buggers alive. There's the aerator, oxygenator, minnow bucket, Styrofoam container, and plastic bag. You would stick them in your pocket if you thought they'd stay alive.

There's real minnow potion you can rub into anything that looks like it can catch a fish. In fact, it would be so nice to catch a fish on this or that product because it's already worked. The manufacturer caught you—the biggest fish is the one who buys a bad product that doesn't catch fish.

BUYING AND TRYING

No one should be critical, including me. Fishing is fun; buying and trying is part of that fun. You see that gimmick, and you naturally picture yourself catching whatever could be on the end of it.

Follow one very important piece of advice: If you can't afford it, let it go. Use what you have, and most likely the fish might thank you for it. Between me and you, make what's due. If you like fishing, anything will do.

Making one's own lures shows a little imagination. A bathtub is a good testing area. If you have children, a bathtub is best. They may enjoy seeing a live fish swimming in the tub Let them play with your catch before you take the fish back or before you clean them.

But your little ones might not want you to take their pets out of the tub. *Rub-a-dub-dub, don't move my fish, bud.* On second thought, unless you really need a bath, leave the fish until your children are asleep. Then clean them.

SIGN AND STRUCTURE

Now, when you do find the time to fish, the first thing to do is look for sign and structure. You're not going to see fish physically very often. It does happen, and if you happen to be around thank someone bigger than you. Look closely to see what they are feeding on, quickly tie that on, and cast. A feeding frenzy does not last long. Hurry, take advantage! How often does a person get to catch fish one after the other? You feel lucky, I guess. You are lucky if you do this very often.

Now, you're looking for a sign and you see a swirl in the water. You can cast to it to check it out. Cast past it if you're using any type of lure. Your chances to catch are fifty-fifty to none. It never hurts to try. If you're in a boat, comb the shoreline for underwater structure. On shore, do the same. Any structure is a good place to start. A bass fisherman especially checks out the shore when bass are nesting. The big mamas are up for grabs if you know how to tease them or threaten their nest. Every fish in any water is voluntary at one time or another.

Now this book is going to jump around a little, the reason being its author doesn't know what he's doing. It is his first book. Now, at my age, don't expect too many more.

AN ENEMY NOBODY NEEDS

Don't you believe serenity and your favorite fishing spot are the two most enjoyable things in your life? Yes, we already discussed the thousands of dollars in equipment, lures, and such. But if these things don't give you peace of mind and fun, you've lost what you should be living for. Fishing should place you in that serene area. The calmness within oneself that comes with doing something you love, like fishing, is all you can ask for. You don't even have to catch fish to place your whole being into this feeling. If you're a person who has a hard time conquering stress, don't stop trying. Fishing cannot hurt your efforts, believe me. God, I believe, does smile on fishermen. You've heard the old adage, "Keep your friends close and your enemies closer." Well, take your enemy fishing. If it's just a matter of any apology, be man enough to swallow a little pride. We will talk about stress several times in this book. Hear me well: Stress is an enemy nobody needs.

TROUT FISHING

Trout fishing is not meant for everyone. The thing is, you don't have to use a fly. I've found a light outfit and a small crank bait can catch several fish. Light line is a necessity. I would never go over four pounds, depending on what I'm after. Always, always check your drag before you fish. That one thing should be a habit. Adopt that one habit if you haven't already. Your reel's drag will tighten when not in use. If you lose one fish because of it, that's one too many. Always try to focus your fishing attentions on your area and on what you are trying to catch. I carry a small tackle box and a few lures with me. I like a light, six-foot rod and an open face with six-pound line. There's always a chance there's water near to romance.

YOU HAVE A FEELING

When you go fishing and you're looking over the water from the shore or the boat, do you ever get the feeling there is a catchable fish nearby? The water is calm and you see no play, yet you can feel something. No, it doesn't make your hair stand up, but you feel something.

It's not that you're psychic. It is a feeling you have developed on your own that only holds for things that satisfy your curiosity. Of course, fish don't bite on your feelings. But for you or anyone, this feeling can be a start. It's like looking for structure you can see. It can be structure you can't see, and you're checking the area around you, looking around bushes on top that continue down to the water. You don't have to be psychic to know there are bushes in the water, too.

I've been in tournaments where the same people always came in with fish. I do believe they have a feeling on the conditions, the water clarity, and what to use to catch fish. I used to call it luck, but how can the same people always catch fish? Yes, they have the confidence. I believe they can feel what has to be done to catch fish. I just have the feeling I'd like to catch some fish to weigh in. That's about as far as my instincts go.

TOURNAMENT FISHING, PART 3

Back in the day, you had to be a member of Bassmaster or meet qualifying criteria to become part of your state's six-man team.

If you did get on your state's six-man team, you could qualify for the national tournament.

Being one without means, I always had to draw for a partner from the pool of B.A.S.S. members who had boats in order to compete in state tournaments. I made the six-man team by two ounces, thanks to pure luck and good boat partners. I'll never forget my friend, Pat Finley. One year, I drew a person named Pat Finley in the state tournament. What a coincidence! I had fished with him before.

I believe it was a two-day tournament to qualify. It so happened I was on fish during the practice days, so I felt good. The first day, I weighed in a couple of fish that put me in tenth place. That made me feel good, but it was a far cry from getting on the big team.

Well, I told Pat I was on fish. He also told me he was on fish. This conversation took place on his boat. In those days, he could go wherever for half a day and I could request my draw to take me to a spot or two. The boat owner usually got first choice. Pat asked me if it was okay to fish his place first. That was nice of him to ask me first. Usually, that is not how it goes. The boat owner typically takes it for granted that they control the first half-day.

I told him it was okay by me to fish his place first. I should make this (apparently long) story short, but for me it was an eye-opener. We were on the Mississippi River, and Pat took me to an old pit area. You had to back up your boat to jump the side bank to get in. When I first saw where we were at, I asked Pat how he was planning to fish the pit. That's when he informed me we had to jump the bank to get in. "Hold on," he said.

My thinking on the subject was: *Let me out of this boat.* But if you leave the boat, that disqualifies you from the tournament. So, close your eyes, hold onto your seat, and say a short prayer.

Next thing I knew, we were in. There were already four other boats in. *How many bass could this pit hold?* I was thinking this to myself, of course.

Not far from the jump, there were a couple of bushes in the water. They were the only ones left without a boat hovering above. Pat asked if I had a white spinner bait. It just so happened that I did. He backed the boat up to the bushes so I could fish first.

What? My mother wouldn't do as much!

I looked at him in awe. What a man! Full of surprises! He then told me to drop my spinner into the bushes and lift it out slowly. There was no room for him to fish the bushes, so I got first chance. I dropped the spinner bait and—*wham*—a four-pounder came up with the hook in her mouth, the first fish on!

I told Pat it was his turn, but he declined. "Go ahead," he said. "You need two more".

Two more it was. Then, he replaced me and caught one bass and that was it—four fish and no more. I will never meet another Pat in competition. As far as I'm concerned, he is one of a kind. If I had an idol, he would be up front.

THIS SWIM FIN WITHOUT A BRAIN

If you love to fish, how many books and magazines do you read about it? As for the fish, well, they don't have an opinion and refuse to reply. Well, I missed one that big and another broke my line. Well, sometimes that is a line. I guess it's like any sport—you think you can beat and outwit a nitwit, and then this swim fin without a brain beats you at your own game.

GOING A LITTLE FURTHER

There we are, looking up at the full moon. The barometer. The temperature. The pressure on the surface of the earth. A true fisherman gives thought to all the new gadgets and will try anything that gives him some advantage. Now, doing all this doesn't mean you're not having fun. It just means you will go a little further to catch that elusive Big Fish.

Those who can afford it charter boats and take along a fortune teller and a diver. Any means can be the name of the game—but not catching fish is an awful shame.

THE CONSERVATION BOAT

You heard the story of the man fishing with dynamite? When the conservation boat pulled up, he threw him a lit stick and yelled, "Go fish." I have only experienced good conservation officers.

OLD-TIMERS AND PATIENCE

The old-timers will cut up their own bait. Their strategy is patience. Now, that's an acquired virtue that has passed a lot of us by. For instance, when a large bass is on her nest, you won't find me patiently dropping a bait and waiting for an hour to entice her to bite. I have been with fishermen who do that while I'm eating a sandwich and sucking down a beer. When they yell, "Get the net," you're not going to see me dropping my beverage. You better be able to mouth that mama.

Just joking of course—I'll never be that critical.

DEEP-SEA FISHING

Who wouldn't love the opportunity to go deep-sea fishing? I'd guess fifty percent of us don't get the chance. The closest I get is with waders in the rivers and streams, trying to catch those big salmon coming in—the ones the deep-water fishermen missed. Now, if this book sells, I will go deep-sea fishing. It would be an experience, and I think I would enjoy it—whether I catch anything or not. I can picture myself hooked onto this big chair with a rod and reel I can't even lift.

THIRD TIME'S THE CHARM

No matter what the situation, I love to fish. I've caught fish that weren't much larger than my bait. Then, of course, whoever I'm with snaps a picture before I can throw it back. I'm being blackmailed by at least three other fishermen.

I brought in, once upon a time, a bass that was just a hair under 15 inches. I took him off the hook and threw him back. I could see him just under the water, but he didn't take off. No big deal. He was swimming, so I figured he would take off in a second or two. I threw my spinner out again and brought in that same bass.

I told my partner, "This is the same fish I just released."

He said, "Are you sure?"

I showed him that I had caught the bass on one side of the mouth. Then I showed him that now I hooked the other side. He laughed, saying that was kind of funny. I released him for the second time. I placed my pole down to pick up a pork rind bait hanging over the side, so it would not stiffen. The real pork baits need to be in the water to keep them soft. I didn't have any rubber ones in those days. When I went to pick it up out of the water, that very same bass hit it, and I caught it for the third time. Now that's hard to believe, even for me, but it's true.

TOURNAMENT FISHING, PART 4

I do like tournament fishing, but most of my boat draws haven't given me many partners who wanted me to come out in front. In fact, many would ask if they could stay in the front of the boat, running the trolling and casting a spot first. No big deal—I could catch fish from the back if it was meant to be. As I repeat, fishing is fun. Never get discouraged.

PART OF THE FUN

The best part about fishing is you can come off the street with hook and bait and start fishing. You're going to find water somewhere. You always want to ask first, though. There will be times when you approach the water and a house, a dog, or something else is in the way.

How much do you love to fish? That is a fun question to ask in that moment. You need to psych yourself up to pass a large dog. Repeating, "Nice dog, nice dog," doesn't work all the time. I believe, for nourishment, fishermen and hunters should carry some jerky with them. You never know when you might run out of bait...or when you might have to just run. Now, is that part of the fun? It depends on how the story ends. I have had my pantlegs tested for strength.

THE ROUND TOSS NET

Have you ever experienced the round toss net? It's a net with a rope at the top you pull on to help close the net after you toss it in to catch fish. It is lined with weights on the bottom, and as you gather it you throw it in a circle.

I tried it crossing my fingers, to no avail. It was the hardest thing for whomever, not me of course, to cast that net so it would open and close on some unsuspecting fish. Now, it does take practice. I would look on while a more agile fisherman tossed that devil net. It would open every time.

It was fun to watch—you could see all types of swim items caught in there. If I could, I'd cast that net from a pontoon boat. Now, don't you think that would be a fun boat to fish out of? You can barbecue your catch! You can also relax on your extended chair with your line hanging over the side and a beer in hand. I'm not saying you should have beer in the boat—maybe just a couple to celebrate a good catch. Who wouldn't like to cook and eat on his boat? If it rains, you can be under an overhang. There are several advantages to fishing from a pontoon. No matter your age, a pontoon can be fun.

THAT BLOOD-SUCKING, SWIRLING SON-OF-A-BEACH

Let me go back to bait again, this time a leech. That blood-sucking, swirling son-of-a-beach that catches every kind of fish. Walleye is its pride, but no other fish can be denied. You have to like this bait because it opens the door for several kinds of prey. Not too many fish can pass up this swirling, whirling, and twisting tasty bait. Put that tidbit on a red hook and a fluoro-carbon leader and you're in like sin. If there's a fish within a trolling mile, your face will hold a smile.

HOW FAR ARE YOU WILLING TO GO?

Don't ya just love fishing? What in your imagination won't you do—that's legal—to catch a fish? I'd even take my wife with me just to hear her tell what I'm doing wrong. How far are you willing to go?

THINNING OUT A POND

How about the guy who uses three twisters on his line? I guess a fish sees the first, likes the second, and hits the third. Well, more power to this guy. He is usually not the type to release a bass. He's after food, and everything is open game.

Today, buying fish to eat is not so cheap. It can put a tap on your finances. If you have a poor-paying job and a couple kids to feed, that makes fair game of anything that is good for human digestion. I normally would not eat a bass unless I caught some from a pond where they are stunted. Fishing ponds where they are not growing because of low food supply are places to supply your pallet. You will not see, in my personal experience, a lot of these ponds. Thinning out a pond is a different type of fun because it makes your mouth water. Nothing like fish for good health and blood cells a-plenty. The building of corpuscles helps build your smaller and much-needed muscles. You can't pull that Big One if you haven't the power. I think Hercules said that in his book: *Don't Trust a Redhead.*

PUTTING RELIGION AND FISHING TOGETHER

Do you think the Pope ever gets to go fishing? I realize this man is worshipped by millions, but maybe just a few hours to go fishing. You know, I think he's not allowed. He may want to go too often, and others are tightfisted with his time. He's allowed to cast a few blessings, but that is where it stops. I'd love to have him as a partner on my boat. If he is as close to God as I think he is, I'll buy a bigger net.

When putting religion and fishing together, you have to go to the far side. You will see once in a while—not too often—on TV a fisherman making the sign of the cross. Our Lord did step into the boat with His twelve apostles, and their luck increased a thousand times. As a matter of fact, He stepped out of the boat and walked around—and the boat was out in the water, not that close to shore.

NO FISH BONES ABOUT IT

Make no fish bones about it, fish can and do feel and hear sound. A fish jumps out of the water, and he becomes free game (invited to supper, so to speak). That's where the buzz baits, spinners, and so on come into view. A bigger fish likes to hear that a smaller fish may be in trouble, thus making him an easier meal. Some of these lures are clickers, knockers, and swivels—and just plain irritating. I don't know if they just make a fish angry or if they're just the supper bell. Reading any kind of fish was never one of my better skills. I go along with other fishermen when I write; if it works, I'm in.

One good thing about a buzz bait is its versatility. You can cast into grass, weeds, atop scum, and around structure. I have seen guys work one, and it's not fair. They have the ability to throw it into the middle of hell, and their line comes out without a neck. When I do it, it wraps around a limb or gets stuck in the shoreline somewhere. I'm the one you're cussing at when you snag on another line. Now, don't throw this book away just yet. It can have some merit if you can read past my mistakes. Sometimes an open mind can be a good sign. What will be, will be—you'll just have to wait and see.

VEGETATION

Vegetation is usually a hiding place if structure is scarce. When I look for some, sometimes there is a tree lying underneath. You know a hundred thousand fishermen have been there before you, yet it still calls to your instincts. You could be the one who gets lucky. They say fish will return to their hangout. Some fish are most definitely caught more than once, bass especially.

If you come across a turtle, nine times out of ten there's a tree limb under the water. Under that limb is a fish, eight times out of ten. Now, all I'm writing is good only if someone hasn't already been there and caught your prey. It's the old saying, "Should have been here yesterday".

WATER TEMPERATURE

They say to put a question mark on them, water temperature is a key. I'll put my finger in the water, and that's as far as it goes. There are times when a good fisherman can't pass up warmer water. Some fish accumulate in these conditions. Why does something that doesn't have brains enough to stay out of the water care? Some fishermen have figured this out, but it's beyond me. I take it for granted. It is like being in a house that's warm when the temperature outside is below zero. Some species of fish you can count on being in warmer water. Bass fishermen measure water temperature when the spawn is on to catch big-mama bass. Water temperature at this point should be in the sixties.

NOTHING WRITTEN IN STONE

Of course, there is nothing written in stone when it comes to fishing. I don't believe too many cavemen with a bone hook tied to some hemp, riding a log, came back to write about their experiences. They were more the catch than the catcher. Back then, anything swimming was bait. You talk about catching the Big One! You're not going to weigh that one in if you did. Hang that baby up on a scale. You would have to be Mr. Muscle to even bring that one in.

FISHING WITH WOMEN

I do like fishing with women. Sometimes the opportunity presents itself. It seems they possess a different outlook on fishing. They like to fish and aren't as competitive. The conversation has more flare. For one thing, you don't have to yell, "Get the net!" When you have a fish on, they seem to get to a net faster than a man. Men seem to hold a little more contempt if you're catching more fish than them.

Don't leave me out, I'm in there.

HE CAN SEE YOU COMING IN 30

Do you like fishing in crystal-clear water? I don't. If you can see a fish in 10 feet, he can see you coming in 30. I like a little tint in the waters I fish. It really doesn't matter that much, just personal preference. A fisherman can catch fish in any condition. We all like to believe that.

CHAIR-MOVING FISHING

I used to love nighttime fishing from the shore. An old folding chair and a small bell on your line in case you get too comfortable. It has been said that fishing from a chair never gets old. It's the old who are sitting in the chair.

One thing I do hate is the little ones nibbling at your bait before a bigger fish gets to it. In those cases, I will not catch a small one. I mean, you're sitting there falling asleep anyway, might as well wait for a larger fish to make the mistake and take your bait. Of course, I'm a line mover—usually from left to right. I'll sit and wait, but then there's this urge to move my line, so I'll pull it in and cast it a little more to the right. I think the fish I'm looking for has a community project there. You should really let the small fish hook up and leave them there to catch the larger one.

Soon I'll fold my chair and move farther down. I might have to crawl over a few downed trees, but there is always a better area just waiting for me in the back of my pea brain. Thinking back, I have to be the most non-sequential, chair-moving, casting fool you'll find in the unpopulated area. I'd talk someone into going with me, only I don't need to make more enemies. I would usually do this fun, chair-moving fishing alone.

Gather around and watch the clown, folding his chair up and down.

THE BIGGEST MISTAKE A FISHERMAN CAN MAKE

The biggest mistake a fisherman can make is to think he knows what he's doing 24/7. Even a pro can pick the wrong lure. Yes, you always have it in the back of your mind that you're going to catch fish. But, as the old-timers say, "It's not fishing if you always catch fish."

I DO LIKE CONSERVATION PEOPLE

Me, I have an open mind. What lengths won't I go to just catch a fish? I'm open to anything legal. That's in case this book sells and gets into the hands of a professional. I do like conservation people. They always have smiles on their faces when they check me out. They have never have caught me with too many, only because I always have too few. The main thing is I'm enjoying what I'm doing.

I knew a couple conservation people who were just top level and friendly. You have to talk them into giving a ticket, unless what they caught you doing was too far out there. A while back, can't say actually how long it's been, I was fishing from a boat close to a fish-cleaning station. I was called over by one of the conservation people I knew to look at a crappie an older gentleman was cleaning. I use the word "gentleman" loosely. It had to be the biggest crappie I have ever seen. It was most definitely a record. I asked the old man why he'd be cleaning a fish so large it was one for the record book. His reply was simple: "What do you think? I'm going to eat him."

It makes you wonder how many nutjobs are out there, cleaning record fish. How many Cuban families have eaten a bass I'd like to hang on my wall? The current world record, caught in Japan, is 22 pounds. I don't think the fish was glowing when they caught it. Oh well, have to sell a lot of books to go to Japan. I'd rather fish close to home and fail miserably with a smile on my face. I've never needed to break a record to enjoy fishing. I would like to

34

see on my line a 10-pounder. And if I got it in, I'd be smiles for a week. I would decorate my wall in a beautiful fish color, maybe open-mouth off-white with the picture.

A GOOD TAXIDERMIST

Finding a good taxidermist is like looking for a good doctor. You want your fish to look like it has just been taken from the water. It is not an easy task. It takes a person with a lot of experience— another pro, so to speak. You can find one out of the phone book, but you'd better talk to people who have experienced his talents before. You might want to take a little time to go and see some of his work for yourself. It sounds like going to an extreme, but it will be well worth the effort. I hate to see a good fish look like a piece of scaled gray hooked to a board. Today you just need to take a picture of the fish before you release it.

Then, there is the question of what you want to mount it on. Driftwood or a natural piece of walnut are best in my opinionated opinion. I've been to the river's edge to look for a nice piece of driftwood. The day I catch that fish I've spent a lifetime looking for, I'll be ready. Don't set your Big Fish expectations too high. But you should like to see your success on your wall for your grandchildren to see.

THERE'S THE SNAGGER

Like I said before, some people are natural fishermen and others are snaggers. I lean more toward the hook-a-limb type. I so envy the guys who can drop a hook between a mess of limbs and come out with a smile. You'd think after all these years I'd learn that technique, but to no avail. I know what they were whispering when I drew a partner: "There's the snagger." That's all right. I can take a jab or two—even a thousand. But stop with the threatening letters!

I LOVE LIFETIMES

I came from a poor environment, and today I still catch myself looking at the cheapest equipment. I will tell you this: Do not buy cheap under any circumstances. If it means only buying one instead of three, buy one. It will be worth it in the long run. And always check the guarantees—I love lifetimes. Of course, there will be several stipulations, but take it with a grain of salt. No store cares to have a grown man at the front desk crying loudly. It may take some practice, but don't look down on success. It works when you want your money back instead of another faulty piece of equipment.

NO RULE AGAINST BEING OVERLY FRIENDLY

You want to know something? I'm not shy when it comes to learning about the area and lake I'm about to fish. I've been known to knock on a door or two close and ask, "Do you fish this area?" and "Can you give me a few pointers?" You're going to find the person who likes to talk fishin'. There's no rule against being overly friendly. It's surprising how many people who grew up around the place you're going to fish want to talk fishing. You're not looking for a high percentage though—just one will suffice. You can meet some very nice people. I've even had one or two want to take me out for a cast. That doesn't happen very often. Just once reminds you that you live in a free country and that people like to help.

I love the United States and most of the people in it. I'd like to see just anyone walk up to a door in some other countries and not get shot. In most places, the doors are not locked. People are friendly and outgoing. If you're stuck out on the road, there will be someone who will stop and ask if you need help.

BAITING FISHERMEN

I saw a lure the other day I would have taken a bite of myself. I realize the lure companies bait the fishermen, but this specific lure sure had "sex-fish-appeal." I still like the shiny, jigging whatchamacallit with the triple hood on the bottom. You can jig it up and down from the boat above structure, and something might bite, or you could snag something. Now, if I snag a fish, I would throw it back. I mean, you can picture me doing that, can't you? I never take unfair advantage when I'm fishing. I'm a sportsman, not a phone-wielding executioner. You stick one side of an old phone wire in the water and the other side a distance away, then wind the old phone up. Whatever it shocks comes to the surface. Then you proceed to net it. I hear of people doing that. If memory serves me, I think I witnessed that very unsportsmanlike procedure once—from a distance, of course. You might ask how far a distance it was. I guess you would have to use your imagination. People like that are incorrigible I'd say. Me, sitting at a distance, of course—just a witness, mind you.

POWDERS AND MIXTURES

Now they have powders and mixtures you put in your live well to keep the fish alive for a tournament weigh-in. I always like to throw in a little weed to keep them active. I'm willing to share for a happy and healthy fish.

TAKING YOUR REELS APART

Have you taken your reels apart to clean? You should once a year, if possible. I do and then I take the parts to a repair place, just to have them check my work. If you have good equipment, I say you can't be too cautious.

WHAT COULD GO WRONG?

When I buy a rod, I like one piece. Something could go wrong when you're putting two pieces together. That's just me.

What could go wrong? Every time I go fishing, I ask myself that same question. Like a Boy Scout, be prepared. I make a list of what to do when I go fishing. I mean, *lists*. I never know where I put the last one. I should make a list of where I put my lists. "You can't fool an old fool," said the fool who wasn't fooling.

I REFUSE TO DROP MY SANDWICH

There have been times when, while eating my sandwich, I've set my rod down and set my click. It never works for me because I refuse to drop my sandwich. It does work for other people, though. When I'm in the boat, I ask the other person to watch my line while I'm otherwise busy. They look at me funny at first, unless it's someone who knows me. They soon realize the type of character I possess, and they are patient. I like patience in another person. That builds character—the character my character never characterized.

THE JOKE IS ON YOU

God, do I love to fish! By now you're wondering if this book is a joke. Well, I'll be completely open with ya: It is a joke, and the joke is on you if you're reading it and thinking it has any merit. As for me, I'm not a serious person, and I like a good joke. I know there will be someone out there who knows where I'm coming from, where I've gone, and now realizes I'm lost. That sums up my provocation from these words of prose.

I love to entertain and this, I hope, is in that category. I do have a fondness for stupidity, and I show off every time my hook becomes untied. So what? Haven't you ever missed putting your line in the right loop? Well? It's not like I do it all the time...and anyway it's the kind of line I'm using. Too smooth.

They do sell those knot-tying things, but I could never learn how to work one. I believe they call that a learning disability. Was my mother right, or what?

IT JUST LOOKS FISHY
Now I'm going to divulge my most hidden secret about the art of fishing: Dress comfortably. You last longer, you feel better, and you increase the joy of being wherever you cast a line. A fish doesn't care if you're in the attire God gave you. It's a matter of feel. If you feel good, you fish well. If you feel overly proud, go in the nude.

I like wearing shorts, weather permitting, and I always wear a hat. I don't know why; it just looks fishy and covers my bald head. And when I'm in a boat, I always look back so I know my way back. Never works for me, but it could for you. There is an instrument that tells you where you've been, where you're going, and how to get back. I do know the sun comes up in the east and sets in the west. That's as far as I got in the location department. There is a North Star, but I'm always facing west. I guess that is a start.

IT'S NICE TO HAVE FRIENDS
When I go fishing with the guys and we have had a bad day, they have me hang my feet over the side. Then we pick up our limits. They can follow the oil slick back to the same spot from the day before. I think that is the reason they let me come along. Man, it's nice to have friends!

MY BAG OF TRICKS
I have a large fishing bag I carry along. I like different-colored line and every size of lure. I have a hundred lures in plastic

containers. I get this by copying others. If I try to think of these things on my own, I get headaches. If you have a headache, you *are* a headache. I carry a rain poncho in my bag of tricks. It has holes in it, being as old as I am, but I don't care. I just like fishing in the rain. Rain hitting the water is relaxing to me, and it is a relief on a hot day.

I KNOW THE STARE

I bend my hook to the left or right, depending on which way my pea brain is rolling. I think it gives me an edge to always have a sharp hook. I carry a small stone just for that reason. Then I have a couple beers to get stoned (joking, of course). I carry more than two when I have my fishing bag in the back of the boat beside me; it puts the back about five inches deeper in the water. I believe the man in front has to lower the trolling motor 10 more inches. So what? They love fishing with me. They never have to say it; I can see it in their eyes—you know, the glare. I'm so wanted by all. I can tell—I know the stare.

WORKING YOUR WAY UP SHOWS SPIRIT

When fishing you can focus on the good time you're having and temporarily forget the bad times. Everyone has problems in life; if it's not your teeth, it's a bum knee. What I'm trying to say over and over again is do something you like to do a couple times a week at the minimum. We all need to relax and let our bodies and the feelings we're holding inside have a moment of silence. As for me, I go outside and try to find a spider to step on. Sometimes, at the right time of year, I'll look for a four-leaf clover. When I find one, I've usually already stepped on it. Now, that's bad luck! When the man said, "If you don't have bad luck, you would have no luck at all," he was looking at me. How many times have I cut off the line because there were nicks, then ended up tying my lure to the line I just cut off and throwing my lure overboard, only to watch it disappear? I look at it this way: If you're a downer, it is fun trying to get it up. Working your way up shows spirit, and you want to own a lot of that.

WATERPROOFING

I waterproof my tennis shoes just in case I might need to stand in the water for any reason. I will also spray my hat. I spray my dog and cat and, on occasion, my wife. If you want to sleep outside, spray your other half. She's very understanding, but she puts her foot down on waterproofing. What can I say? I'm a spray-can addict. I don't have any paint brushes, just spray cans.

AT THE WATER WORKS FACILITY

Now there are phones that take pictures. I know this because my wife got me one to keep track of me. It takes good pictures, too. I have several of my pockets.

I would have liked some pictures of the bass I used to catch when I was sassy at the water works facility. Back in that day, you were not allowed to fish there because of the liability. I'd sneak through the woods to fish it. There was an elderly gentleman who drove around to chase anyone dumb enough to trespass. When I heard him coming, I'd hide unless I was fighting a big bass. Then he'd catch me and warn me of the consequences. There were always consequences, but sneaking in was part of the fun. I figured I could outrun him anyway.

I can't tell you how many times the Big Ones would pull me in the sticks and weeds and break off. I believe the record then in Iowa was 10.3 pounds. I could be wrong. I do know I lost some big mamas.

A PAIR OF WADERS

I finally saved up enough money to buy a pair of waders. It was not to be, though. The first time I used them I walked through the woods. A tear was there—all I could do was swear. I wore them anyway; I wasn't about to let them go to waste. I'd get glue and the old innertube patch. Those waders had so many of my patches, I decided to bring the whole innertube and ride it.

BETWEEN YOU AND MOTHER NATURE

You think it's not scary when you see a snake coming your way?

When it comes right down to it, the real contest is between you and Mother Nature. When she spits on you with thunder and lightning, it can make you think about your future fishing trips. Waving a rod in the air with lightning nearby is a challenge only an idiot can respect. Sure, try to scare me. I'm up to it. Or is it, I'm down for it?

You can't take the fisherman away from the bite. Well, you can. But like I say, an idiot will always be up to the challenge. I have put Mother Nature to the test, and she did respect my stupidity on more than one occasion. Today, no way. I want to live to fish another day. It's funny, but when you're young the contest is on. When you're older, you don't feel that strong. Your movements are not that strong, and your age is slow. Who cares, if you're enjoying what you're doing?

THE CASTING HERO

It can be so sweet to see the water ripple as the wind blows past your face. You're already prepared to cast when a fish jumps and the minnows fly. You cast to that very spot and miss by four feet. Yes, that's me. My hands don't exactly follow my eyes. I won't admit that in the moment; I just call it becoming excited. I never did win a casting contest in our club. You think these guys would have felt sorry for me and let me be the casting hero just once. They offer to buy me a seeing-eye dog instead. What kidders!

TOURNAMENT FISHING, PART 5

When we had our club tournament, I'd pull out a six-pack of non-alcoholic beer and put a can in a coolly. I'd make sure they were watching; then, when they weren't looking, I'd switch. It can be little things like that that make your day more fun. The non-alcoholic cans look a lot like the alcoholic ones.

We gave so much money per man for first, second, and third place. I never won, but I did take in big fish once. I was catching some small fish on this one lure and, sure enough, I lost it. I asked the person in the boat with me if he had one. Sure enough, he did. I borrowed it and caught a big fish. He wanted it back, but he wasn't willing to chase me for it. That's part of what I love about fishing—the friendly experiences.

I met so many great guys when I was half awake at 5:00 a.m., before the tournament started. You wake up much quicker when you put that first lure on the snap and the treble hook goes into your thumb. That's always an alert feeling. And you know you're too old to be seen sucking your thumb. I'm not a 5:00 a.m. person, as you can see. What's wrong with a 10:00 a.m. start?

There's nothing like a good day of fishing to make you realize you're still a child at heart. I never want to grow up. What's in it for me if I do? Just responsibilities? Now, I ask you, what fun is that? Who wants to be responsible when you could be fishing?

WORTH AS MUCH AS GOLD

I really believe fishermen live longer lives. They have this need to stay around to catch the Big One. It makes no difference what you're fishing for; it's all in setting that hook and just wondering what you'll get this time. You could get lucky. Just being able to go out and enjoy the day, I feel lucky. You can catch a bluegill or a crappie on every cast, and on every reel-in you wonder what will happen next. And if the next fish pulls harder than the last, this wondering turns into excitement. That is what fishing is all about. The child comes out and age goes out. That feeling is worth as much as gold to the one who loves to fish.

WHAT YOU SEEK IS WHAT YOU GET

There will always be one advantage every fishing person holds: You don't need to fish. You can enjoy the moments just sitting offshore and watching the life and the movements of the frogs, turtles, beavers, and muskrats as they play. The activities around different waters can be exciting and raise the spirits of almost anyone. I've had the opportunity to fish under a waterfall and ride the river on an old truck tire innertube. Most of the time, I walk and carry the innertube until I find a hole deep enough to fish. You don't know what you'll find in deeper water, but of course you really don't care. Anyone would be happy just being able to fish in this manner. On a hot day, dripping wet, your course has been met. What you seek is what you get, sometimes.

WHAT COULD ANYONE HATE ABOUT FISHING?

What could anyone hate about fishing? Let me rant.

I hate it when I find the right spot after looking for a year, and it produces. I catch fish one after the other and throw them back, over and over again. I'm alone and haven't shared this secret place with anyone, mainly because it's fun to be by my lonesome sometimes.

Then, one day, I find another fisherman in my secret spot. He's loading up. When I go back, he's there with a couple of his friends, loading up. Doesn't that itch you the wrong way?

I hate it when you're fishing and Mr. Buts crowds in. Next thing you know, you're snagged on his line. To make things worse, he's using 100-pound line and breaks you off!

I hate it when you're anchored, and Mr. Buts comes across with his boat. There go your lines, down under.

I hate it when the dummies toss their empty beer cans in the water and you have to pick up after them. They are the ones who force pond owners to say NO!

It makes your stomach ache in a no-wake lake when a boat flies by, making everything shake. You're going to mouth your big bass on your knees, and here comes Mr. Buts, flying by on skies. There goes your bass, swimming away, in the wake from the skier's breeze. Good-bye, bass. I wonder how many skiers are fishing people?

TOURNAMENT FISHING, PART 6

Wow, I'm having such a good day in the tournament! I'm calling fish. This is a dream come true.

I lift a couple of fish out of the live well to throw the smaller one back in the lake. How easy can that be? A one-armed man with only two fingers can do it. I lift both fish up and go to throw the smaller one back in the lake. The bigger one flips, and in the lake it goes. Great, I lost first place by two ounces.

Shake your head and grab your nuts. You just lost the tournament with a fish short on guts. God, do I love fishing!

DAYDREAMS

Wouldn't it be a dream come true, retiring and being able to afford a place to live where going fishing is daily exercise? To make it perfect, you would always catch fish. Unless you win the lotto, it's no more than a wild wish. You really don't realize how many daydreams are involved in making good fishing a reality.

Yes, the magic is in the fun of the catch—but it's even more in what you catch. You will never catch the Big Fish because you and I will always think there's one much bigger out there. And we are correct in that line of thinking. The only thing that is going to stop you from catching your dream fish is your dream fish coming to life and eating you. Only then will you truly be through. To be truthful, by now, you know I just like fishing.

NEVER DID LEARN HOW TO SWIM

It's funny—or not—but I never did learn how to swim. I tried, but I was told by someone—whom I can't remember—that I was a sinker and that it would behoove me to be able to hold my breath and paddle and pound water profusely until my efforts moved me closer to land. I found I could dog paddle with a lot less effort, so I took this child's method to heart. If it's not too far to safety, I could, theoretically, save my own life.

GIFT-WRAPPED

Life can be a piece of crap, and all you can hope for is that it's gift-wrapped. You do not want to find it wrapped with fishes at your door. That might not be too bad if they were cleaned, though...

SKIN-PULLER AND SCRAPER

When I was young, I did most of my fishing on Sunday afternoon. It was nice if I had a string of fish to bring home. Mom would sometimes help me clean. She was not a fillet-er. Instead, she was more of a skin-puller and scraper.

THE PULL, THE DRAG, THE PUSH AND SHOVE, AND A LITTLE LUCK FROM ABOVE

To a true fishing person, it makes little difference where they fish or what they use as long as they are there and healthy enough to drag out a large fish. In my youth and catfishing days, I would do that very thing. I would hook up with a larger cat from shore, not wanting to lose that sucker. I'd back up and literally drag him on land. In those early days, it was more fish than fight. Nowadays, I enjoy the pull, the drag, the push and shove.

ON THE MIGHTY MISS

I do like river fishing. The Mississippi is one of my favorite places.

On the mighty Miss, you never know what you're going to find: how many species of fish, plus other run-around shore marauders. I was bringing in a three-pound bass when another fish like I've never seen before came up and tried to eat it. It must have hit me wrong, because it actually scared me at the time. It was time to move it; it was getting late. Was I really scared? No, I added that for flare. Do you think a fish can scare someone of my caliber? Come on now, is the Pope Protestant?

You can find a lot of places to fish along the Mississippi: locks and dams, pit areas, and small ponds and small lakes—they all hold their share of fish. In these conditions, I like to use a steel leader. Some of the fish of interest have teeth. They have even been known to show some interest in a trolling motor blade.

I love my fishing, but back in the day, I don't know if I would have jumped at the chance to fish in a canoe. In a tree-bark boat, I think my name would have been Running Chicken.

THE WORD "FISHING-TROUBLE"

The chance of choosing the right lure was about nine out of ten. When the area was on, so were the fish. I liked a spinner bait with a trailer hook. There were so many times the fish just wanted a taste and weren't interested in takeout. The chance to catch so many kinds of fish was worth the trip. The people I'd meet living along the shore were an experience in friendliness. I would even receive an invitation for shore lunch. I believe I may have mentioned that before in this Class A writing. Just the people you happen upon while fishing makes all your escapades worth any trouble you may have. When you're fishing, what is trouble? I can't find the word "fishing-trouble" in the dictionary. Fishing the Mighty Mississippi was an experience and always has been.

AN OLD BARGE ON THE MIGHTY MISSISSIPPI

Sometimes on the water, you find an old barge parked that, for some strange reason, holds a fish or two. Some of the barges have been parked in the same place for who knows how long. Those produce if you have a little patience.

A true story: I had just gotten to the weigh-in at a tournament when this other boat, running late, started mowing down barge waves, trying to get in. I could see it was a new boat, and the guy running it wasn't planning to lose any ounces by arriving late. He raced to the weigh-in area by traveling between a moving barge and a dock. He hit the oncoming barge waves so hard he split his new boat in half. I would have laughed, but it wasn't a bit funny. He lost all his gear, along with his boat and motor. A couple boats rushed out to try to save something, but no luck!

As for myself, I stretch my imagination, but not my luck. My luck is so tight you can't even stretch it. It has very low tolerance on both ends. When I carried luck in my boat, it was under lock and key. I never did find that dang key! Luck has always evaded me. What is luck any old way but a state of mind? Mine has been out of state for a very long time.

FORGETFULNESS

I keep a lot of my fishing stuff in the boat for one simple reason: I'll forget half of it if I don't. There's been a couple times when

I've had to return for my wife. Thank God on both occasions the lake wasn't too far away. Then there was the time I forgot my boat. I didn't find this out until I went to unhook it and it wasn't there. When I got back, my wife was still sitting in it and had eaten all my sandwiches. That was the last time I didn't take her fishing.

FLY FISHING, PART 2

Fly fishermen: You can't miss them. They advertise wearing hats with little bugs on them. They carry a 30-foot pole with orange line and are always licking their lips like something's going to happen real soon. I've never met one who doesn't enjoy swinging that large pole around.

Some of the more independent fliers, with the complete fly-fishing attire, tie their own special flies. Why go through so much trouble when you can swat some horsers? I don't know how they do it: How can you see that teensy, weensy, little fly? Maybe that's why they keep licking their lips: It keeps them sharp and ready to set the hook when the water boils.

You've got to give them credit when the fish are on. They don't keep it secret. They're blabbermouths, and you'll see them lined up in a row jabbering with one another. You would believe they have a secret society when they aren't fishing.

I'll tell you another thing: When they hook something big, like a large salmon, all of the ones close by bring in their lines and give the hooker a free rein. No animosity there. They like to watch as well as catch.

One more thing: They all run to shore to get a long-handled net. Like a net race. Depending on where the fish comes to shore, you'll find someone standing there with a net. This can make you a believer in what fishing is all about.

CREATURES OF HABIT

Ya know, I've watched a thousand fishing people, and all of them are a little different in their approach. You've got the spit-in-the-water-before-fishing ones. The ones kissing their hook and even their bait, rubbing their line, and other places, before casting. Each person seems to do his or her thing before fishing. This may not be so obvious to the naked eye, but it's there. We are creatures of habit, and we all do some things a little differently. That includes fishing.

Now, I can tell you I'm not the best person to go fishing with because I'm a complainer. I'm the first one to pitch a bitch, but being so good-looking and such a personality-plus, people just seek me out and want to hang around me anyway. Not everyone can be perfect, so I have to feel sorry for everyone else.

TEACHING THE ART OF FISHING

One of the best reasons for going fishing is taking a young one along and turning them on to the most fun they can have for the rest of their life. If I had the funding, I'd teach the art of fishing to the young and the old—from the shoreline to the water to Heaven, from the first cast to the last, how to share. A parent should always take time to be there to teach his or her child something every day.

MULTI-TASKING

Are you a canoe or a kayak man? I never did care for just reaching over the side of the boat to put my hand in the water. I prefer a little distance between me and the surface of the water. If I'm going to fish with a finger or an arm, I prefer it be someone else's. Believe me, I'm very careful mouthing fish in the Mighty Mississippi. Once, a fish as big as the boat tried to eat the two-pound bass I was bringing in.

Why do they make nets? I wouldn't want to put a net-maker out of work. You've got to look out for the other guy. Anyway, my favorite words are "Get the net!" When I get into another person's boat, I yell those three words out just to see movement. If no one moves, I'm in the wrong boat. I don't care for the nets with push-in handles. If I see one, I have a habit of pulling it out and placing it near the hand of the other guy for luck. Anyway, what respectable fisherman can't hand-board his own fish or net it? I don't worry about such things. My fish I can throw onboard with four-pound test line. I see fishing people who can heave a six-pound bass into the boat with little to no effort. I'd need a 100-pound test line attached to a spring to copy that move.

Now I'm not trying to indicate I have trouble doing everything—just anything. As long as my legs can move, my hands can grab, and my eyes can see, I'm going fishing. When it comes to fishing, I've found you do not need to be good as long as you can pay someone who is. If this book sells, I'm going to accompany someone who can fish and doesn't care who he's with. Once you get past the cussing, kicking, jumping, and missing the piss can, I'm really not that bad to fish with. I have my moments, but who doesn't? I do enjoy teaching a young one how to fish. If you can get them to bait their own hook, the man upstairs will smile on you.

Well, back to kayak fishing. It amazes me how a person can paddle one of those with a pole up on either side, trolling for a fish. You have to appreciate their abilities. I mean, I can pick up a fork and knife, but paddling a boat and looking to catch food that's not already on the plate...more power to them. People of that caliber are to be looked up to; they have passage and a place.

NO ONE LIKES A SHOW-OFF

There are some sights I can't figure out. You'll see line, lures, etc., in trees, power lines, and other unbelievable places. You know it's not a child because I can't imagine a young person casting that far. I hate seeing that because I'm usually the one who snags into that mile-high line. It's only when I'm not paying attention, of course. It could be more often than I am willing to admit—my memory is a bit foggy in those situations. What fun would it be to make good casts ninety-eight percent of the time? I can tell ya, I must have held my own in place casting because the club members always asked me if I could refrain from casting in front of them. I may have caught onto their lines a couple of times. No one is perfect. The only reason I never won a club casting contest is because I didn't want to be a show-off. No one likes a show-off, so I was well liked.

BORROWING LURES

I'd like to touch on borrowing lures again. There is nothing wrong with this friendly idea. I'll loan one out. Sure, I'll ask for it back. Yes, I have a personal rule: If you lose mine, you owe me two. Sure, no one ever asks to borrow my lures, but it could happen. If I ever get enough money together, I'll pay for all those lures I've borrowed and lost. I can't believe my club made a rule against the loan of lures. Now, if I remember correctly that rule had my name on it. The guys are such kidders. A person can't carry every lure a fish is biting on. I only have a twenty-tray tackle box, but I do keep the proper colors and nothing older than ten years. I think my other borrowing rule, of giving me a fifteen-dollar deposit, is not too far off. The guys never ask me, but it could happen.

PASSING ON THE BULL

In our bass meetings—being the good fisherman I am, as you can read—I make awesome suggestions. The club members put these great ideas to a vote, and there are times they come close to passing. The one I made about borrowing a life vest was turned down, but I know the reason is all the other members can swim. I'm going to take lessons someday.

I mean, swimming is not a skill you're going to use every day. I can hold my breath for at least 20 seconds. I can get a long way dog paddling in 20 seconds. I did buy an orange vest at a garage sale for 50 cents. The guy wanted 5 dollars, but I just knew he'd come down to 50 cents. I've found that, after a discussion, most people come around to my way of thinking. I love haggling. I've never met my match; people seem to see things in my favor after a length of time. You would think I had bad breath or something.

You will understand by reading this that I enjoy passing on the bull. To think on it, it's not that easy to write a book that's eighty percent farce. There could be something educational, but that is in the eye of the beholder. If there is something to be found, I want all the credit. There are times I even amaze myself. I haven't been amazed in a long while, but who's to say what the future may bring? There could be a song in those last statements—if I could sing. Even whistling is not my forte. I'm the one who enjoys watching people with talent. I can juggle one orange at a time. The only reason I don't do that is I eat it too fast. My main talent is not having any.

BEING A GOOD GUIDE

There is such a thing as common courtesy in fishing. The hardest thing to do is permit the guy with you to join you up front when the stump you're fishing holds more than one fish.

Every time I do that, the guy I'm with catches the bigger fish. Now, what is that all about? I think it could be attitude, but I'm such a nice character. Can it be down to just that?

I think the one up above meant for me to be just a guide. You have to take pride in being a good guide. Like I mentioned before, one stump can hold many fish. Never forget to come back to it. I will draw up a map so I won't forget. I just wish I could remember to bring the map. I have several at home somewhere.

Well, anyway, it is so much fun to fish a bush or a stump and trees that hold more than one fish. You can just sit back—pole in one hand, beer in the other—having a lot of fun. Not that I would ever drink and fish. That is not a good thing, and even I know better.

JERRY

I have to repeat myself: Don't ever, if you can help it, turn down the opportunity to go fishing. It helps clear the head, the stress, and the aggressions. There's never a bad day to go fishing. I once worked with a guy who would sneak off in the middle of his shift to go, and I would cover for him. The foreman would ask, "Where's Jerry?" I would say, "He's in the restroom or something." After several times, the foreman would ask me to get him. I'd look around, but to no avail. Thank the stars Jerry was so good at his job; he produced more than anyone, and the foreman would turn a blind eye. Too bad Jerry was a fish-eater. He had a time with the catch-and-release aspect of the sport. That didn't turn me against him. We had our times.

THAT STUMP DISAPPEARED

Back to structure fishing. I went to this small lake that had a huge stump, way out in no-man's land, that held big fish. You could never tell what you were going to catch. Well, the little lake only held bass, crappies, and bluegills. But they were big. Every once in a while, I'd lose a jigging spoon when it dropped too low, but it was definitely worth every lure. Over the years, that stump disappeared. If I'd found it, I'd mount it. I mean that in a preservation way.

WE ARE OPPOSITES

I have a close friend named Larry Goodmanson. He gave me permission to use his label. I love fishing with him, even though we are opposites. He is usually a jig fisherman. Why he fishes with me, I can't tell you. He has patience—something I never learned. If I'm not catching something every other cast, I'm gone. He's so relaxed while waiting for that next bite. I can't tell you how he does that, but he does catch fish. His outlook on life in general is...well, I can say he doesn't have an enemy. Me, I collect all kinds: big ones, tall ones, dog ones, and such. Most of the time, when he has me sitting in one spot, it does pay off. I could learn from him, but I've never tried. I'm glad he will never give up on me. I call him brother. Always wanted a brother, but I had three sisters. And, of course, they don't fish.

A PROBLEM WITH CLARITY

Do you have a problem with clarity? I do! When someone asks, "Where did you catch all those fish?", I try my best to be direct. But the clarity of my speech and direction is not the best. I believe I have a problem with memory, too. When I give the place and area, sometimes the individual will call and say, "Ben, you must have caught most of the fish. Our luck was terrible." Now, I know I didn't send them on a wild fish chase intentionally. I think I must have a learning disability. I've got to get that checked in the near future. God only knows I have very few secrets. My escapades are held in high esteem, not to be heard of and never again to be seen.

I DO WONDER ABOUT THE OTHER GUY...

I love to fish, as you can read. River or lake, fast or slow, pond or hole: I never discriminate. Put me there, I'll fish anywhere. If you're lucky to find someone to fish with, you have been blessed. I will call around for company, but everyone is so busy. I do believe it is because I never give back the lures I borrow.

Busy. I'm familiar with the word, but the idea doesn't in the least motivate me. How can anyone in their left mind be too busy to fish? It can calm a lot of nerves and push a lot of good buttons. Over the years, I've met a lot of fishing people and never talked to a negative personality. There's an outlook on life and good intentions that are a sought-after and preferred commodity.

It seems the older I get, the more I want to run my mouth. At times, it's not easy to find anyone willing to keep up with a runaway mouth. I love to talk fish, and there are times I find someone willing to listen. The secret is to let them think you know what you're talking about—not an easy task, really. My biggest problem is that I'm talking a lot faster than I'm thinking. There could also be a lie or two in the conversation; not intentionally, I can assure you. I do wonder about the other guy...

UN-GATORIZED RIVERS AND STREAMS

When I'm fishing on a flat-bottom boat on a warm day, I enjoy taking off my shoes and hanging my feet over the side. I don't fish around gators; I value my toes. I've heard there's big bass in places like that, but who wants to catch a big bass that bad? I do want to catch big bass, but who catches who first?

That's a question that requires thought. Can you imagine catching a gator on a hook? You won't be calling for the net, I betcha. I think I'll stick to un-gatorized rivers and streams; they produce much safer catches.

THE MOST POPULATED BAR

I've got another tidbit for you: When I'm in the nearest town to where I'm going to fish next, I hit the most populated bar. I'm not one to pass up a cold beer or the fishing conversation that might go with it. My intentions are selfish, but that's followed by picking the wrong person to receive my beer ninety percent of the time. I'll take the ten percent though. Ninety-eight percent of the time, you'll get a beer in return.

By the time I leave the establishment, I've lost four or five hours of fishing. Two to three hours to return home: There goes the fishing, but I made contacts for next time. You can't beat that for the future. If I could only remember the next time where they said the fish were. I'm going to have that learning disability checked when I remember the time after next. I can't be too cautious with brain farts, or farce, or something to that effect. I may repeat myself in this book several times, but don't mind me. My brain does have its ups and downs and all arounds. That's always been of interest to me because if you don't know what you're doing, you're not going to be a failure.

ALWAYS LOOKING OUT FOR NUMBER TWO

I'm not an energetic fishing type, but I have seen one or two fishermen walk the bank and climb over limbs and trees to fish. I try to save all my strength for casting. When this individual comes back with a stringer of fish, I yell out, "So you caught a few fish." They almost always say, "Yeah, I had to throw some back."

Do you just hate those guys? I hope they get a hole in their waders.

Not really, they have my respect. I'd do that very thing, but I'm satisfied with my talents wherever I'm at. The reason I don't catch multiple fish is that I'm always looking to the next guy.

I leave quite a few fish behind for that very reason. I know by now you look upon me as one extraordinary man, but what can I say? You're a credit to your opinion—I'll give you that. I'm just a humble person looking out for all who like to fish like me. That's why I don't try too hard to win money or trophies. I'm always looking out for number two.

See, Dad and Mom, from up on high, how you raised your son? I know you're proud. Don't be bragging to any angels. I found my place on this earth, and I learned to eat humble pie for breakfast, lunch, and supper.

FISHING SHOWS

Now, back to fishing. I can write a complete book on just how great I am, but that's just not the nature of this beautiful beast—I mean, extraordinary animal with pages of meaningful suggestions.

Fishing shows: I like to watch some of them, while others are for the rich and famous. I'd like to watch a down-to-water fishing show where the boat pulls up to the trees and the guy gets out with a roll of toilet paper. No one catches one large fish after another all the time. I have a hard time believing people who like fishing would find a program that showed a person catching fish every cast enjoyable. These people have to lose a fish once in a while. I do it more often than a while and not only once.

Being on a fishing show would be a great opportunity to be wicked and catch tuna worth thousands of dollars. They can keep half the money—just put me on to a tuna fight. I would need just a few extras, like a waist float, life vest, and an automatic blow-up pair of waterproof diapers. That's very little to ask for, I think. I'm such great company that they would ask me back. I might consider it, but no promises.

One older show I did enjoy was the Virgil Ward show. He was so down to earth and didn't mind live-baiting his hook and wiping off on his shirt or pants. Of course, today that is grounds for a divorce. One thing I really never minded was cleaning my catch. However, this book isn't specifically true to life; there could be a lie or two.

I would love to have my own show and actually get paid for something I love to do with no cost to me. I wouldn't need make-up or that sort of thing, being so naturally good-looking. A million women can't be wrong (just thinking ahead).

Just think of all the people you look up to who you could invite to go fishing. If dreams came true, who would ever want to wake up?

I do go a little far in pushing fishing as the greatest pastime. You would think it was my lifelong passion. That, of course, is an observation. Don't even give that a second thought. I just enjoy the sport a little.

Going back to having my own TV show, how many people would have to watch to make such a thing feasible? Plus, I would have to find companies willing to contribute. Now it's getting complicated. I'd be so happy doing the show for free. I bet I could find people to come on the show for free: a real-life fishing show. Who needs a hundred-thousand-dollar fishing boat? As long as I never have to fish from anything low in the water; I'm not one to reach into the water for temperature anyway, again I say.

One other advantage of having your own fishing show would be the free gear. I wouldn't need to buy any more bad choices: All I'd need to use would be given to me. I'd be somewhat famous, and my picture would be used to sell things I couldn't afford and now can get for free. Don't you love that word, free? Has a ring to it, and it doesn't cost me anything to use in what I love to do (fish).

It is all really about the advertisements. If the show doesn't sell the product, it will soon be history. The product has to show an increase in sales after the show starts. A show on fishing can go on and on, depending on sales and entertainment. What would not be entertaining about some clown like me showing viewers what not to do and how easy it is to look funny fishing? On the other hand, such a show could be accepted as a guide on how not to make the same mistakes.

EAGLE PETS

Have you ever gotten to watch an eagle? Not your own, which only flies when you feel a little high. The proud-winged type. They can be up there in the sky, then they suddenly dive to pick up a fish. Wouldn't one of those make a good pet? It gets fish, and it doesn't bark. I could have fish in the freezer and eat one for breakfast any time I cared to—only for a little corn, bologna, and left-overs. I'd have to hide out in the country somewhere and change my name to Jeremiah Johnson. They look down on eagle pets.

There goes the eagle fish-catching idea.

MEMORIES I NEVER WANT TO GIVE UP

Whether they're good, bad, or indifferent, don't forget your memories. If you're reading this, they can't be all that bad; if you're reading this bit of prose, they can't be all that sad. If you weren't reading this, you would just be watching TV.

We do learn from our mistakes, and that goes for your fishing prowess as well. Fishing is a fun activity where we can all have an unforgettable experience of some kind. If you're lucky, you find and catch fish. If not, you find snags, lose lures, and break line.

Like when I fell in that hole with my waders on. I beat the water so hard I sent waves up and down the river for miles. The unfunny thing was my Massey buddies knew it and laughed at the possibility of me drowning. We used to go fishing and occasionally spend the night on the weekend. These guys were crazy, and I miss them. They would do anything for a laugh— usually at my expense.

These are memories I never want to give up. Most of them hold a place in my heart. The reason for making that stupid remark is this: One of the jokesters in our group carried stick matches. You'd think he was a fire bug, but he fit right in with us crazies. He'd light a match, put it behind him during a big one, and it would flare up. He thought that was so funny! I thought he was dangerous myself. I kept a distance.

We did have fun. We'd have a campfire and talk most of the evening away. Some of the troop would bring jingle bells and tie them to the tips of their rods. We talked so loudly after a couple beers, who heard the darn bells? Above the river there were pits, and it was private property watched by highway patrol. On the weekends, sometimes groups of college students would swim in the nude. I never did—never had nothin' to show off. At times when we were fishing, we could hear the partying and would go up top to join them with some of our beer. We were always welcome with a cooler of beer. Today that pit property is a pay-to-swim area. How times do change. I think they have built houses not too far away now. I can't remember what I ate yesterday, but how can you forget the fun times and memories?

THIS BAROMETER THING

I knew this guy who was a barometer, pressure-o-meter, psycho-to-meter, fishing analytical, fish-by-the-pressure-gauge freak. He would not go fishing unless it was written in the stars. He read his weather gauges, read the news on better fishing times, and wouldn't go unless everything pointed to catching fish on that specific day. He read his horoscope to follow up on all possibilities. He was eccentric; but then again, he caught fish. I do believe we all have an angel, and his loved to fish when he or she got the chance from their host. I never could figure out what the make-up is of an extraordinary fisherman. I repeat, I had the fortune to know a couple who could catch fish in a sewer opening. They don't smell fishy, and I use the same bait and lures, but they catch more fish. I want their fishing angel; mine falls asleep.

Now back to this barometer thing. There is atmospheric pressure hitting the earth, but can you believe it affects fishing that much? I think it has some bearing on fishing, but I can't for the life of me figure out how much. In truth, I really don't want to know. I want to go fishing whenever I feel the urge. I learned about trying too hard in my years of almost always coming in with low numbers. A winner I'm not, but a fisherman I'll always be. The only forecast I look for is whether the fish are on. Come and get 'em!

JUST GET OUT YOUR TACKLE BOX AND POLE

We live longer, don't you know? Fishing is the way to go when your life is running slow. Just get out your tackle box and pole, and away you go. You could run into someone you know or just go with the flow. God made you to follow in fisherman's mode.

Fishing is a take-a-chance sport. Use every opportunity to go, but know you're taking a chance on being successful. What I'm trying to tell you is to go out there and suck up the fresh air. We all need a little fresh air for our health. The freshest is blowing across a body of water. You will never find polluted air blowing across a lake, out in a field pond, or along a river. Fishing outside will always be healthy until some idiot pushes the Big Button. Now, that will happen when I'm fighting my dream fish. We all need to say a prayer every day and that never happens.

If we could take every world leader fishing together on a large boat, I bet they would make friends. Can you picture them, comparing fish and sharing? The only disagreement could be an ounce or two. Can't you just see that happening? All the equipment would need to be identical—no advantage anywhere. Our Lord walked upon the water to let the apostles catch fish, indicating we will never starve; there will be fish to feed all. I do believe a higher source had something to do with man's beginning.

BACK TO GEAR

How long do you think that spring-loaded, red-and-white bobber has been around? I can tell ya I've kept that invention alive. I've broken, cracked, and lost 6,432 of those—along with line, hooks, and one tennis shoe in the mud. I think the company should at least give me a new pair of low-quality tennies. The one I lost was cheap and may have had a hole or two. When I couldn't buy waders, I wore old shoes.

I don't know why I'm going back to fishing gear; it's the little things that bug me. I used to get away with bending a rod before I laid down my moola. I'd bend it back, and if I didn't hear it crack it was a keeper. Nowadays, you touch the rod against something to see if you can feel the vibration in the rod handle. When I have an extra dime, I love to go shopping for anything fishing-related. I like buying what I don't need in case I lose what I borrowed and never returned.

There's the string. They have so many types in little rolls and large rolls. Some easy to see, others no one or nothing can see. They advertise that not even a fish can see your line. I know they're trying to get me away from my 100-pound string. I purchased a rod once where the string went through the middle to the reel, like a tube. Today when I go to buy string, its eeny, meeny, miney, moe. There are boxes and boxes of all kinds. I want to buy a box with a fishing guarantee: You catch fish or they'll give you a certificate for a box of store fish. Can you just imagine? That company would have to hire people to open all the mail.

You used to get to pull the string wrapped around both hands to see how strong it was; now, you're not allowed to open the box. And reels. Now they have slip clutch, release so much, are light to the touch, drag and lag, tight low sag, ultra mag, aluminum, titanium, afradanium, ingcrum, positivium, and then some. I was getting used to the reels where the handle went backwards and painfully knocked your knuckles. That is a wake-up call. Now with the reels today, the handle doesn't go back a twinge. They have these no-slip, easy grip, fingertip rubber covers. I'm waiting for them to put a phone number in the reel box of a person who will take you fishing as a free guide.

They have come a long way with the sport, and I can't say I disapprove. A lot of the gear is out there to lure the fisherman, and you will find me in line. It won't be long before the reel has a phone and the rod is an antenna. You'll be calling a friend when fishing is good. You'll be able to call a guide for a price, and he will give you directions. You'll be able to take pictures with your reel.

WHEN THE FEMALE BASS IS SPAWNING

I don't care what they do to make it easy; fishing is fishing. It's nothing like hunting. The hunter stalks his game and knows that, in his own sweet time, he will kill his prize. In fishing, there is one time when a fishing person will do something similar, except they also catch and release.

When the female bass is spawning on her nest, we will stalk her and try to get her to bite. This can take some time. Once caught, ninety-eight percent of the time she will be released after a picture. I tried this once, only I was always too early or a little late. I need a fishing friend to call me when I can catch a hog.

If I wasn't so cheap, I'd pay someone to be my friend. I've borrowed too many lures and equipment to keep a friend. I forget that borrowed things are to be given back. I do give back what I break. Now, you can say that's kind of a breakthrough with my borrowing problem. I will do better in the future whenever I find someone to loan me something.

I just remembered that when fishing for the big bass at nest time, you use a rubber worm and preferably a black rubber lizard. It would be nice to have a live crawdad or two. If you go to a bait shop, don't expect to find the creatures alive. You need to be near the right lake or river at the right time. You'd think I could find a kid who would catch those baits for me. I might even give the kid a bubble gum or two. When I was a kid, what wouldn't I do for bubble gum—besides work, of course.

BUILDING PATIENCE AS WELL AS CHARACTER
I'd be the first one to take a kid fishing, especially if he had his own bait. Any time is a good time to take a young one fishing. Training a youngster to fish is more fun for me than them. To see the look on their face when they catch a fish is worth more than money, gold, or other such things. You can't buy happiness. You can't buy the feeling you get watching a little one catching a fish. Every girl or boy should get to go fishing a time or two. It can help build patience as well as character.

I LOVE THE SPORT AND CAN'T HELP BUT LIKE THE PEOPLE

I'm going back to equipment again. I haven't found a reel I cannot backlash. Yes, I know. I can cast with the worst of them. But if I set a reel so I don't have a nest, it will only cast 10 feet. Do you think I couldn't do it if I tried?

Well, I did get a little better. I had to because it was that or go back to the Coke bottle with line wrapped around it. To love fishing is to learn every day and meet people like you. There are a number of people who like to relax and fish. If you're not out to beat your neighbor, you're out to join him. Nothing is better than fishing to meet others and talk about your similar interests.

It's like my experiences salmon fishing. You hooked a salmon or lake trout, and there were three others to net it for you. What other sport can compare? Even in competition, if you have boat troubles, there will be someone there to tow you in. They will give up precious fishing time to do so. And when they do that, the place where they are anchored is safe. I love the sport and can't help but like the people.

GRUMPY OLD MEN

Funny thing: While I was writing this, *Grumpy Old Men* was on TV. They're two old codgers, drawn apart and brought together through fishing. There are parts of the movie that are so true to life. There are so very few things that draw us together. I don't mean like an outside concert. Some of those draw thousands of screaming, overly involved children. Fishing consists more of tip-toeing, silent-moving, and sneaky people. It can be hard to come upon your prey without scaring everything within fishing distance. I know a couple of guys who could walk in water without making a splash.

LIFE, LIBERTY, AND THE PURSUIT OF HAPPINESS

Life, liberty, and the pursuit of happiness: In our U.S.A., that holds true. Our conservation preserves the environment, and protection is very important. We need limits on all species. To buy fish in your local store can be a wake-up call. That is one reason for the increase in fishing incentives and live baits. Of course, you'll always have nighttime crawler hunting.

NIGHT-CRAWLER HUNTER

I've always been a night-crawler hunter. I'm just not as fast as I used to be at grabbing the slimy, quick-in-a-second worms. I never like going into my pocket for the cost of a worm. So what I do is fish with the half of the worm I end up with. I think they will get along.

As kids, we had names for yards we'd search, looking for worms. The names depended on how many worms each place gave up. We liked the park, until it became over-shined with flashlights. Today I'd bet that park is empty. People would rather pay two and a half for a dozen nighties. Now I find places where the worm crawls up to the surface, easy places to find them. Collection made easy. Jack's driveway is number one. Park in the street, Jack. After a good rain, the night crawlers crawl up on the concrete, making pick-up easy.

NO ONE IS PERFECT

You know, I don't remember anyone ever saying to me that they were not in the mood to go fishing. Fishing makes the mood. It makes the minutes, the hours, the good times. When I'm not in the mood, it means there's work involved. That mood doesn't move me. Who wouldn't be in the mood to relax on a lawn chair, fishing? You'd be missing a good part of life, and watching others fish can be fun, too.

I knew this character who was moody and had a cigarette hanging out of his mouth 24/7. I think he slept with a carton under his head, no pillow. He'd fish with that cigarette hanging there. The ash would drop, never in an ash tray. Whoever's boat he was in, there would be ashes in the carpet. One time, he had a big one on. Rod up, good fight, and you can guess what happened. Fishing line doesn't take well to heat. Raising his rod to set the hook, his cigarette hit his line. Good-bye, fish.

Now, there's a fight, trying to break a smoking habit—took me forever. I tried to quit by smoking a pipe with cherry-blend tobacco. It burned the tongue right out of my mouth. I chewed packs of gum, even key tobacco, and finally handcuffed myself to a telephone pole. Not good—the neighborhood kids threw tomatoes at me and took my pack of cigarettes out of my pocket. I stopped then. I wasn't going to let anyone see me buy another pack of cigarettes. Today, you can buy two good lures for the price of one pack. I'm too cheap to buy new lures, so you know I no longer smoke. I only spend money on food and candy bars. I do like anything that's two for one. I like anything free. You never see me pass a penny on the ground. I tried to fix a broken fishing pole once to save a penny or two. I think I did pretty well on the repair, except the eyes at the handle end were up, and at the other end the eyes were down. No one's perfect, so I fished with it anyway. My first hook set was problematic, but it was fun hand-lining that fish. Did I say no one is perfect?

A GOOD FISHING PARTNER

It doesn't matter who you have for a fishing partner. If the fish are biting, you won't mind the company. It is wonderful if God gives you someone you truly enjoy. Having a good fishing partner makes every day a good day. Just having something in common makes life a little easier. It doesn't necessarily have to be fishing. Wait a minute, did I write that? I'm getting writer's cramp or mind freeze—whatever.

A BUNCH OF NICE GUYS

Did I mention I like fishing with leeches? I'll buy a dozen and cut them in half so I have twenty-four. There's nothing wrong with more. People have told me you want a whole leech; they'll live longer, and you'll catch bigger fish. Now, what kind of crock is that? I ain't ever seen a fish turn down a leech because it's too small. Sure, I fished with guys who used the whole leech and caught bigger fish, but they paid for the leeches. So what? It's their dollar. I will use a whole leech when I'm with the nice guy who buys the bait. I always reach in my pocket for money to buy, but my partner always beats me to the cash register. They know I'm buying the next time...and the next. I even bought a lure once to replace the one I borrowed. I got it on loan again and lost it. Oh well—easy come, easy go.

In tournaments with the club, you give the guy with the boat a twenty for gas. They all knew I didn't just carry around that kind of money. Most of them would say, "Forget it, Ben. Catch you later." You talk about a bunch of nice guys! When they called for a net, I was on it. I mean, grabbing it. What a twenty-dollar bill can buy.

I RESPECT YOUR SPACE

Don't you like fishing in the rain on a warm day, with raindrops hitting the water? The sounds are pleasant, and the fish don't spook as easy. It's relaxing. I always keep a poncho in the boat. You'd better have two if you're going to fish with me. I'm not one to clutter your boat with gear. I never want to be in the way with more than one fishing pole or a big tackle box. Don't you just hate it when someone loads your boat with gear? Not me—I respect your space. And, anyway, most boaters have enough of everything for two. If I lose or break something I borrow, you know I'm going to replace it. You can ask anyone who knows me—that time is around the corner.

That corner might be a little distance away.

FISHING IS MAGIC

Fishing is magic. You wave this wand, and something pulls you into the excitement. Your thoughts speed ahead when you're fighting a large fish. This is a process that takes over, especially when you've only been catching small fish. You have a bigger something, you don't know what. You want it bad. You want to see it. What is it? So many things are going through your head. Wow, it's heavy! It's moving methodically through the water. It's now feeling so heavy. You're talking to yourself, now saying over and over again, "Get this in. Get this in." Now it's coming up, and you don't want it to jump and throw the hook. Now you can see it, and the excitement disappears.

How in the hell are you going to get that big snapping turtle off your hook? I hate when that happens. If the head sneaker is big enough, I do love turtle stew. After some work with my power saw, you'll find a couple of different meats. Mixed with onion, celery, and carrots, nothing is tastier.

NO FREEZER BURN

Fishing can give you an exceptional diet. Fish are cell-builders for sure. If you're too tired to clean your catch, a few months in the freezer will not hurt a thing. Wrap them up, no need to clean, and freeze. Sometimes, I don't get back to cleaning them for a couple of months. Make sure of your wrap—you don't want freezer burn. Don't you just hate that? Then, whenever you get back to clean them, they taste just as good as the day you caught them.

COMPANY

After a day of fishing, I rest so much easier at night. I'll go over the day, and no matter how bad it may have been I will have a smile on my face. A day of fishing is a smile all the while.

Back in the day, I liked to follow the blue book put out by the conservation people. It gives the lakes in your state and the types of fish in those lakes. It will tell you if there's a boat ramp, a camping area, etc. It's a very helpful little book and good reading. Today, it is a white booklet.

But I will repeat myself again: Talk to people. You will never find an unfriendly face. People who like to fish and camp are the best. Even if you don't know each other, you can sit at their campfire and talk. Most of the time, you have to introduce yourself since most of the campers will talk to you without asking for your name. I'll introduce myself as the best fisherman there. That always gets a laugh. If you don't have a boat with you, it's a good bet you'll be invited on someone's. In cases like that I won't charge too much if they want my company.

DO SOMETHING YOU LIKE

If you can't make a memory every day, you're not fishing. Memories are made of mostly things you enjoy. I like making good memories every day, so I'll never turn down any possibilities. I'm ready for a memory. Grab one, they are out there. Take the time to share. You have only one life to spare.

I will repeat: Do something you like doing at least once a day. Now, if you like washing dishes, I feel sorry for you. I love to fish, but your thing could be golf, basketball, ping pong. Whatever is your fun time, take the time. If you don't do this for yourself, you lose what may identify you and what you need to be happy. Don't ever go through life without a smile on your face at least once a day. You can't help but like a person who smiles at you or who can put a smile on your face. God gave each of us this expression so we can make a new friend, or even go as far as attracting a lifelong friend.

UNSEL*FISH*LY

Over the years, I've had the opportunity to watch so many other people fish. Everyone I witnessed had their own technique. It could be something small that sets them apart. I can read an amateur and recognize a pro. It makes no difference if they are enjoying their choice in pastime. I have never run across anyone I wouldn't go fishing with. Sometimes I'd have to teach them how to fish properly, but I'll sacrifice. That's just the kind of nice guy I have always been. I give of myself unsel*fish*ly. To give someone a chance to learn from the best, what can I say? We were all given something special, but I'm a special specialist. I not only like to cast the bait, I like to throw the bull. If you're reading this, you have figured that out by now.

CATCH AND RELEASE

We all want to catch the Big One, and I repeat: A true love-to-fish person couldn't care less as long as they are enjoying what they are doing. That goes hand to reel with fishing. Catching a fish is fun and releasing them makes you a special sportsman. Fish in the marketplace is a little expensive, so I understand why some people need to take some home for meat. Never, never take more than you need, although I'd take a couple home if I could find someone to clean them. So catch and release is appropriate. When I come across a stunted pond, it's an open table for me.

WHY I DON'T GO DUCK HUNTING ANYMORE

Every pond and lake has a silver lining. I've met many a dog when getting permission to fish a farm pond.

I have a story outside of fishing I want to tell you. It was in my younger days, and the fellas and I were duck hunting. We saw this pond from the road with several ducks, so I went to the farmhouse to ask for permission to hunt. A nice gentleman—or so I thought then—came to the door and asked, "Can I help you?" I said that we saw several ducks on the pond and asked if he would care if we shot a few. He looked at me kind of funny, and then with a smile on his face told me to shoot all I wanted.

I went back to the car and told the guys we were going to be eating duck tonight. We loaded up and started to sneak down so as not to scare any of them before we were in shooting distance. We started walking down a small hill toward the pond, as quiet as we could be. We were getting closer than I thought we could, and not one duck flew away. All hell broke loose as one of the guys started killing anything feathered. I hadn't shot yet because none of the ducks flew up from the water.

Then I saw a truck and car coming up to block our car in. I yelled at the team to stop shooting. A lot of good that did. When the duck slaughter was over, I could hear the mad farmer—the neighbor of the guy we had talked to—yelling in one disturbing voice. His truck was blocking the front of our car, and his wife was blocking the back with her car. Our group was trying to collect ducks when I yelled for them to stop. Guess who had to go up to talk to this very angry individual.

When I got there, he was holding a shotgun and was so upset he could hardly talk. His wife had him give her the shotgun and explained that we had shot her husband's pet ducks. They did not get along with the neighbor I had asked permission from. She was very nice, but her husband was still chewing his teeth. I could hear the grinding. I told her I would try to pay for the ducks. Me being the only one with a job, I came up with forty-two dollars, and we ended up with sixty-eight dollars altogether. She accepted the money and moved the car. Her husband wasn't about to move anything. Seeing the glare in his eyes, we decided to leave his ducks behind; that was the very least we could do. Our duck day came to an end. There was no stopping at the local bar for a beer with no money to spend.

I don't go duck hunting anymore. I'll stick to fishing and hope I'm asking the right person when getting permission to fish. I have never heard of pet fish in a pond, but why chance looking stupid? I can look that way sometimes, but I don't take chances. If I go fishing with someone who said we have permission, I still ask.

ANOTHER TRUE STORY

Here's another true story. I asked permission to fish a nice-looking pond; it had a dock and everything. The guy I asked gave me permission, so I parked my truck as close as I could get to put my little boat on the water. I was on the pond, and my first cast caught a large crappie. Was this going to be a good day, or what!

As I was reaching the far side of the pond, a man exited the house nearby, yelling. I was hoping my great day wasn't going to come to an end. I paddled closer to him to hear some angry words. Hard to believe, but I was encroaching on his half of the pond. He wanted me off and to release my four big crappies. I let the fish go, sadly, and my great day came to an end. I did learn from all my experiences, but how far out there can a man's life reach? I can't cast that far—I can tell you that. I will never complain: My good days are mostly made up of my fishing days. Some of these days hold some surprises, but those surprises make the game even better. If the score is fish one, Ben zero, I'll win the next go around. You can beat the old horse, but you can't keep him away from water.

THANK YOU, PEOPLE OF FISH RULES

Even at this late time in my life, I get excited about going to a new area to fish and discover. In the smaller, older towns, you can find old lures and who knows what else. I love old coins as well as old lures. You never know where you'll find a pearl.

I do enjoy reading the booklet the conservation people put out with all the local information. They show where the lake is located, as well as the size. The booklet lists the types of fish in each lake and if it is accessible with a boat ramp. How much more can this small collection of about twenty pages hold? I give them a hand—even two, so I can clap. Like I said, it is exciting going to a new area. This booklet will let you know if the fish you're after are there. Thank you, people of fish rules. You're the best!

In all my years, I haven't run into one conservation person who hasn't given me a break. To explain, I'd keep maybe one or two bass over my limit to call later. If I'm busy catching fish, I wouldn't break to check size until later. When I was stopped by a conservation officer, he or she understood and let me call the smaller fish in front of them. Never a ticket. They seem to understand and always wished me luck to catch even larger fish. I respect the conservationists; they have never given me any grief. That's not to say there aren't some buttholes out there—maybe one in a thousand. If that holds true, I'll find one. I attract buttholes: B.H.A. degree.

GOD SMILES ON CHILDREN

I was getting gas today and ran across this man who started talking about his grandson, who was going to be participating in the local rodeo. He started to talk to me because he saw the gold hook I had slid onto the bill of my cap (I put two and two together when he continued with his grandson's love of fishing). He went on to say the kid would rather fish than eat. His grandson didn't live too far from me, so that opened the door, so to speak. I had taught a young kid to bass fish tournament-style a year earlier, but his father had other ideas for him. He respected his father so much that fishing became secondary. But I got the phone number from this grandfather and thought maybe, just maybe, I had a future pro on my hands. Between rodeos, that is. It's hard to find a young one who eats and sleeps fishing. I'm willing to devote time and patience to this individual.

A child's mind will find in time a place where he or she will shine. They could be kept away from what they truly want to do by a parent, but sooner or later they will find their own way. They will find a spark that will enlighten the dark. And given time, they will shine. God smiles on children all the time!

WHERE I WANT TO BE

They say there's a place and time for everything we do. You need to find what's best for you. I pick fishing, as I mentioned, for the relaxation and beautiful scenery in so many places.

I had a friend who, believe it or not, loved coon hunting and deer hunting. He was a small person in stature, but he had three sons who were over six feet tall. They loved hunting with their dad; they were children who would wait on him hand and foot. They were hunting together one day, and their dad became tired and let the guys go ahead while he sat next to a tree. He didn't catch up, so they hurried back to find him sitting against the tree with a smile on his face. They thought he was asleep, but he had passed away. The smile on his face, I figured, was because he was where he wanted to be. He was at peace.

That's where I want to be: a fishing pole in my hand and falling forever in a very deep sleep. The thing is, that will be when I hook my dream fish. I won't be around to realize the sensation. Don't you just hate that? If you do, call me. If you can make the call, I can answer. Fishermen live longer, don't you know?

FISH, FISH, FISH—QUITE A DISH

I don't know if I mentioned it, but catfishing is great when you're around them. When you locate feeders, you can pull your boat over them and actually jig them one after another. I've found the best place to fish them is where you find a rock pile or two. I take a lively minnow and follow that with a piece of night crawler. That worm will cover the point of my hook, which is red steel. You can load up on catfish, but I only keep the ones I can fillet. By the way, that piece of night crawler helps keep the minnow on the hook.

I know most people cut, gut, and skin. I realize filleting is a bit harder, but it is worth the effort. I'll take and pull what bones I can and soak them in orange juice and chicken juice for an hour; then I fry them or bake them—it's your choice.

Any dry soup mix that you like can be used to soak your fish for fifteen minutes if you are planning your meal right away. I sometimes melt chicken spice or allspice in butter and pour them over my fish and bake. You're the leader in your own taste! *Bon appétit.*

There are so many ways to fix fish: frying, baking, smoking, and the old, reliable burnt board. I like to put pecans in my melted butter for a different taste. Also good is a baking bag or aluminum foil. The fish will fall off the bones, so to speak. It's really up to you and your imagination. Fish is so good for you, and your experiments will usually come out delicious. Fish, fish, fish—quite a dish. What more can you fish for, if not the very thing that is good for you?

FISHERMEN LIVE LONGER, DON'T YOU KNOW?

Normally, a working person will get to fish maybe ten to twelve hours a week. We all need to make a living, and I agree with that negative way of thinking. Only, I don't care for the work part. Work never did appeal to me over fishing. I will admit, coming from a poor family, I had to work. My dad wouldn't have it any other way. He wore the biggest belt, and it could reach at least 100 feet or more. I could not beat that belt in a race. He was an Italian who married later in life and was set in his ways. You learn to understand this. He was not a fishing person: If he could shoot a fish with his double barrel, that would be the only way. He'd take spaghetti over fish any day.

How did he come to raise a fisherman? That question goes unanswered. I loved him dearly, although he never once took me fishing. His intentions in raising his only name-carrying boy were admirable. He worked hard for his family. When my mother served some of the fish I caught, I think he just took it for granted that they were store-bought. If only I could have gotten him to go fishing...I should have tried. Chicken.

Now, I wrote this book for fun. It was meant to entertain hopefully more than one. I sadly got personal in some areas, and I apologize. Fishing has been good to me. To whoever reads this: I hope you take some time from your busy schedule to go fishing.

Fishermen live longer, don't you know?

PART II

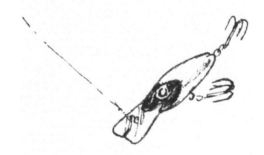

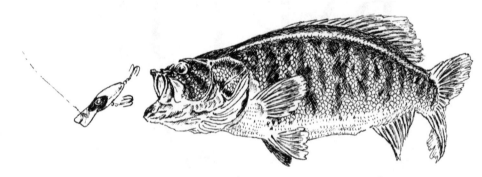

POETRY

I was walking to the pond. I could see at a distance a deer and her fawn. I could hear the frogs singing their song. As I got closer, the sounds of the pond were in my ear, soft but strong. At that time, how I wished my children were around; but sadly, they have grown and moved on. Now I'm alone with no one to share, too many are gone. Did I do something wrong? No, everyone should live as long.

Why would anyone want to leave this earth without living at the least one of their dreams? At the least, life should be a roller coaster with yells and screams, walking distant streams, discovering all you haven't so far seen. You're a human being: Your limits can be extreme, but you can still reign supreme. You may need a team to follow your dream. You're only a human being: Dream, with your family as your team.

I conquered my fears, at times with too many beers. I love the places where there is yelling and cheers. Never cared for sadness and tears. Stayed a distance from that—didn't want to even be near. Bartender, give me another beer.

Now, I hope you understand what I've been trying to tell you. It has guided me in the right direction, so I know it is of value. It will help you renew what you hold true. I would have said nothing, but I find you are one of the few!

If you are reading this, that holds true.

Now, think about it. I know you're discouraged, and the answer is not in sight. But think on it, you'll soon see the light. Say to yourself, "I can with all my might." Control, don't become so uptight. Now you can see the answer was in front of you, clearly in sight. Be yourself, day and night.

Am I just part of the crowd? I want to be heard, not just loud. I don't want to rain on your parade, the only dark cloud. I will speak softly, try not to be loud. Swallow a little pride, not becoming overly proud.

I just had a misunderstanding with a wonderful girl. She's a diamond, not just a pearl. She gave me love, pleasure, and respect. Who could ask for more? My return in feeling was sadly poor. I should have asked for forgiveness before she walked out the door. I hope to see her just once more. I'll explain when I didn't before. Forgive me, just once more.

I could hardly count the telephone poles, my friend was driving so fast. He's a personality who wants everyone to kiss his ass. He believes he's number one—no one else is in his class. He's the bull in the china shop; he breaks a lot of glass. Where do you kiss when he's all ass?

I'd write a line if I had the time. And who would read it? They would have to be one of a kind. Where would I look to find one so prime? And why would I try? I'm not that kind. Forget the line. I haven't got the time.

How do I follow the footsteps of one so dear? He gave me confidence to control my fear. When I needed him, he was always near. Thank you, Dad. You made everything open and clear. I wish I told you that several times when you were here. My heart sheds more than just tears. I'm giving this to you now, so you'll understand what I will always fear: That there will be a day when you're not so near.

I asked Mom and Dad for a puppy. I thought the time was right. They said I couldn't have one until I could go to sleep without a light. Don't they know a lot of boogies come out at night? You can't see them if you don't have a light. So now I want a bigger dog to sleep with me at night. Then, and only then, will I turn off my light. Make it a dog that doesn't bite.

Stupid is where dumb has been. You start out dumb, and stupid is where you end. So look ahead before you begin. You may be dumber than just stupid at the end. If you begin closer to the end, who knows where you have been. Sounds stupid, but starting dumb is where to begin. Do it with a grin.

Let's say you had two apples, added three, and had worms in five. You threw the ones with worms away and climbed in the tree for three more you gave to me. You ate what was left and got sick. Did you get one with worms? Or was it on me you played a trick?

My personal best was better than the rest, no contest. I cold have settled for less, lowered the stress that started the whole mess, but I couldn't care less. Doing that is where I got the stress. What a mess. No, I settle for less.

I'd like to list out some things I've done wrong.

1. I brought a dead minnow to a bass fight.
2. I used two-pound line in an ice hole that was stocked with five-pound walleye.
3. I tried to cast 50-pound test nylon from a spinning reel.
4. I pulled a seven-pounder out of the water with an extra-light rod.
5. I didn't test my hook tie before casting.
6. I bent over the boat to mouth a fish with my fish-tying glasses and sunglasses in my shirt pocket.
7. I cast into a bush with a jigging spoon.
8. I didn't use a leader in teeth territory.
9. I drove my trolling motor into a producing fish bush.
10. I checked the worm on a Texas rig, looking for a point.
11. I found out it is pointless to have a worm with a point.

Sixteen pieces of advice for people who love to fish

1. A live frog should be followed. When it stops, wait ten seconds before catching it. Hook the frog by one leg, or the lips will do
2. Keep minnows alive. Hook them properly.
3. Do not snap nylon string with your front teeth.
4. Use the right bobber in the right place. Have patience.

5. Save money for a fish locator.
6. Save money for a boat to go with your brand-new fish locator.
7. Plan the lake you want to fish, keeping the fish you want to catch in mind.
8. Always have a full tank of gas in a car before you leave, but buy gas for your boat close to your destination. This makes a lighter tow.
9. Stay in an area where the fish are biting.
10. Don't overcrowd your partner.
11. Don't overcrowd another boat.
12. Always check your boat's batteries, live wells, and stops.
13. Return bass back to the water for the next fortunate person, especially if it is big.
14. Carry a net.
15. Take pictures. They are worth a thousand words.
16. Take a child with you and TRAIN them well!

I would fish wherever I could. Sadly enough, some catches weren't so good. But at my age, I was so happy just to be there—knock on wood. I wasn't in a wheelchair and felt 10 feet tall on any shore where I stood. Fishing didn't need to be that good.

I love you my GOD. I want You to know. I know You see all, and I'm not doing this just for show. You've been my constant companion wherever I go. Please keep on protecting my body and soul!

If you are a fishing person and truly love the sport, then you're no longer catching fish. The fish have bagged you. You're the trophy. Your weight is insignificant. You will always be there to see. You're the one with a smile on your face. Keep fishing. Keep up the pace.

This is a wonderful world with a thousand places you can go,
   Places where it's nice and warm, where you will never see a flake of snow,
   Where the fish get bigger and bigger and have more time to grow,
   Where the warm breezes caress your face, and you can relax under the sun's glow.

9 781732 352612